She Sits Up...
After They've Gone

Linde Grace White

Cover design by Chloe Annetts
www.chloeartdesign.com

Published by МEDIACS

Also available as an eBook

Contents

Acknowledgments

Nobody writes a book like this without a great deal of assistance. It would be impossible to mention all my helpers by name, but I will try: The Keefers, Carol Muntz, Jackie Sauers, the jerk from Mensa who date-raped me (a learning experience), Dr. Robert D. Caldemeyer, the therapists I recognized when to say good-by to, the therapists who actually helped, Jucy Little, VOICES in Action (no longer exists), Leah Proctor, Marion Cooley, Rosemary Franz, Jill Gustafson, my brother, Craig Deitschmann, and others who, I hope, know who they are. These are the people who helped me find my way out of the jungle.

I am thankful to folks I met and organizations I found on the Internet. I am glad for the books I read and for people who listened and, at times, cried with me. If you helped, a heartfelt thank you to you. I hope this book helps others as much as you helped me.

Special thanks, hugs, and everything nice to Rhonda Partin-Sharp who read every word three times, proofread, and explained where what I wrote made no sense. She is an editor extraordinaire!

A big thank you goes to Wayne Holmes as well for his encouragement, and to Jim Bergman for taking this on as publisher.

An Unrecorded Nightmare

She sits straight up. She does not scream in the darkness. That has never helped anything. Her heart is speeding as if it could overtake and pass a Formula One car. She stares at the blackness in the room, begins to recognize familiar shapes and deliberately slows her breathing down. She says to herself: "I am okay. I am at home in my own bedroom. I am alone and I am safe." She repeats this mantra until she wakes enough to believe it. Then she turns on the light beside the bed to find that it is all true. "Bad dream," she concludes, slipping into the moccasin slippers on the floor and reaching for the thin ragged plaid bathrobe she might need. She goes to the bathroom and sits, the robe in reach on the floor. Her head swims just a little, nothing to be alarmed about, maybe just the jolt of waking suddenly and getting out of bed quickly. She stands with no problem, flushes, washes her hands, and gets a drink of water. She walks back into the bedroom as if this were just a normal wake-up-to-pee event. She sits on the side of the bed, slides out of her shoes, and remembers what she can in the light, in reality.

She determines that this has not been a nightmare worth recording in the notebook she keeps handy. It is only about a 7 on a 1-10 scale where 10 equals "have to get up, leave the bedroom, write, drink hot tea, and resettle for at least half an hour before going back to bed—even if that means back to bed on the couch for the rest of the night." One means "I just remember vaguely feeling upset." Nights are the worst, of course, fewer distractions, and nobody is likely to phone after 10 p.m. unless it's big news (generally the bad kind, but, occasionally, the good kind, like "She's here! The baby came at 4:10 a.m. Come on down to the hospital and see her."). A seven will wake her up, but she'll recover quickly and go back to sleep. For the several hundredths time, she is pleased that no one is there: no husband, no boyfriend, no woman friend of any sort, and, now, no children at home either. She is completely alone; even God has stepped out for a smoke or something. That's good because it puts her in total control of what happens and that is exactly what did NOT happen all those years ago.

The thoughts come unbidden at any time, day or night. She can distract herself if she starts out awake, but the triggers are everywhere. She never knows when a forbidden word might be said, even on TV or radio. She doesn't know what another person might say. This is one of the major blessings of living alone, staying out of groups, and being in charge of the remote: she doesn't have to listen to it. She can talk herself out of obsessing on the "bad" words and ideas, but that takes time and she resents having to use that time for such a purpose. She could be doing something creative with her mind and hands. She hears others lauding their families to the heavens, and anyone within earshot, and has nothing to say. She often wishes she could squirm in those situations or yell "Shut up!" but that's unacceptable in polite society. So she likes to spend time alone where she can manage whatever comes to pass.

It isn't that she's not proud of how far she's come or that the children she has raised to adulthood are not completely wonderful or her grandchildren are not the most handsome, talented, and clever children who ever graced the earth. They did not endure the abuse she did. She made definite and concerted efforts to prevent that, feels successful in that effort, and does not cling to them. She is, one might say, defiantly independent. She is always glad to praise the generations below her on the family tree. It's the ones above who caused all the problems.

She speculates about what would have become of her life had there been no abuse. No doubt it would have worked out better, but who can say how? There are plenty of success stories of people who have overcome amazing obstacles to emerge, not normal—they and she can never be what many consider to be normal—but able to cope and salvage some happiness and satisfaction. She considers herself a success. She achieved education, a fairly good career, and those beautiful children. She can handle herself in society, often by assuming the appropriate mask, but nevertheless functioning in an acceptable manner. She knows who cares and who doesn't. Although her ability to trust is almost non-existent, she can generally rely on some folks, especially when she thinks about what is in it for them. The man at the store wants her repeat business. It doesn't pay the water company to put out a contaminated product.

She seldom thinks that somebody just likes her even when that person gives all the signs that that is the case. This is a mistaken carry-over from a childhood where she was an object and not a particularly cooperative object. A Barbie doll does not complain or have opinions, nor does it feel pain. It accepts as right whatever the owner does to it or thinks about it without judgment. In fact, it has no feelings, thoughts, or opinions. It is an object. Walt Disney has taught all of us to think that objects have personalities, but they don't. Barbie just looks cute, wears the clothes, and does what the owner wants Barbie to do. There's no harm done if you leave her, arms and legs akimbo, upside down in the bathtub overnight. She is different. She has difficulty remembering she is a person. She has learned "people skills" by studious observation, book reading, and research. She paid attention in college and graduate school. If Mother did it, it might be wrong, so beware. She got her facts. You must get your facts.

Does any of this connect to you? Have you had similar feelings? If so, I invite you to read on.

If You Are Just Beginning Your Journey Out

If you are at the start of your journey, first, be thankful. Something or someone has helped you in some way. Even if it seems that you did it completely on your own, someone or something gave you the impetus to go on. Those women in Cleveland who were imprisoned by a sexual predator for over ten years are thankful that when the opportunity came, there was someone out on the street who stepped in to help. Jaycee Dugard, when she was finally able to give a sign, is thankful for the campus policewomen who picked up on that sign and helped her get free. Someone or something has helped you to break free. For me, it was my own unexplained depression. I had extensively studied child abuse for my teaching license and my counselor's license, yet I did not connect what I learned to my real life experiences.

When it became safe to do so, my subconscious mind started to work on the problem. My life was pretty good though I was depressed. After all that education, I wasn't sure I knew what to do. I consulted my doctor, rejected medication (eventually found some to be helpful), and saw a therapist. It still took 6 months to begin to crack the surface of my issues. I am thankful that the therapist did not think I was just another whiny middle-aged woman complaining about how badly the world treated her. A huge part of recovery is recognizing and accepting that there is a problem that you can no longer live with.

You may feel ashamed at this point of the journey. After all, you've been told thousands of times that it was your fault this happened. You have no clue, of course, as to what you did to cause it. You do not think you are worth the trouble of healing, that it's probably too late, anyway, and there is no hope of any kind of satisfaction. One of the things a good therapist can do is help you re-frame your experience so that you conclude different things about it.

Your experience will stay the same, but you will change. You will begin to see yourself as a strong and capable person. You might not have been able to see anything positive in what happened to you, but that experience is a motivator. It is the opportunity God (the Universe, your Higher Power) is giving you to become the person you should be now. You will not forget it. You will not, after therapy, think it was okay or that you got what you deserved. Therapy is not brain-washing. It is facing reality and choosing a different response.

One of my realizations in the course of therapy was that everything my parents did was not wrong. I wouldn't say that they are absolved from the truly horrendous things they did or that I would welcome a reunion with them (can't happen anyway, they've died), but I can say that many things they did were all right or neutral. Even a stopped clock is right twice a day. I can recount positive events and focus on the positive aspects of others.

Here's an example: my mother loved to sew, and she was very talented at it. She made beautiful clothing for me, but complained greatly about my body not being perfect for the things that she was making. She had to make adjustments and it seemed accusing to me as if I could decide to have a symmetrical body. I must say, in my defense, that my body isn't grotesque at all (another thing I had to re-frame). When I think about my mother sewing for me, I focus on the great wardrobe I had, the always appropriate outfits, and the compliments. I remember the pleasure it gave her. I can sew, but I don't enjoy it much because my mother criticized my sewing, and even re-sewed a garment I was making for my daughter. I have very little interest in fashion. I am usually happy if what I am wearing doesn't attract any attention, keeps me warm enough, and doesn't give me any mechanical problems. I could focus on the complaints, the endless fitting, and the frequent lack of choice in the garments I had as a child, but I have chosen to focus on the positive. You may be surprised at your ability to do this. You will likely be surprised and pleased at how well you coped in the first place. Give yourself credit for all the things you have done right. Make a list if you need to.

In starting out to heal, you not only need to recognize that there is a problem, but you have to have some definite goals in mind. This information can be pretty murky at first and may require adjustment as you go along. I was a teacher for many years. When you are a teacher, you have to "begin with the end in mind." What do you want your students to be able to do or to know at the end of the lesson? What experiences, exercises, or steps will you set up for them to lead them to the desired conclusions? You will be taking one step at a time, and, yes, step one might be "open book to page 3" or something equally simple. You can't just say, "I'm going to teach children to read." You need to take into account the current level of the children's reading ability, the age of the children, things that will interest them and motivate them to want to read, the materials you have to work with, the children's preferred learning mode, and so on.

I taught a child to read whose mother had told me early on that no less an institution than the Children's Hospital Medical Center here in Cincinnati had assured her that Kevin would never learn to read. She was elated when I sent reading homework home which he proceeded to read aloud to her. Kevin learned to read, in part, because I let him land and clean his imaginary plane before we started.

It's true that not every teacher has that kind of time. I just ignored his need to duck under the table two or three times to clear out the imaginary sewer. When he bobbed up, we went on. My goal was not general. It was specific to this child. Step one, in this case, involved merely getting the kid to come to the reading table and open the book.

So, what kind of specific goals might a sexual abuse survivor at the outset of the journey to healing have? You will have to decide for yourself, but here are some suggestions. Choose the ones that you think will help you to make up your own or mix them up.

Hint: making the perpetrator sorry and apologetic is NOT a good goal. This would be an amazingly rare outcome. That is why you only see it on the news once in a while. If this happened all the time, it wouldn't be news. Do you really want to see headlines saying your family had chicken for dinner on Thursday? No. The only way that would be interesting is if there were something truly shocking and unusual about it.

The perpetrator is highly unlikely to think he did anything wrong--he blames you for being cute or whatever. He will use any means, including apologizing and "making it up to you" in order to continue controlling you and having your body at his disposal. The perpetrator is only interested in himself. He sees you as an object over which he wants to exercise total control. The chances of a perpetrator feeling genuine remorse or regret are remote. You can, for all practical purposes, take that idea off your expectation list. You can only change or control yourself and your perceptions and never anyone else's. Here's the list I am going to work from in this book:

1. Lose the fear(s) — these will vary somewhat, but range from physical fear to psychological fear, and, usually, a mix of these.

2. Develop self-esteem — recognize the goodness in you and dwell on that.

3. Learn who can be trusted — be firm in readjusting the company you keep.

4. Move the perperator into a new position in your life. If you had to lose a limb to save your life, you would never forget that limb, but you would adjust to the loss of it, learn to do things a different way, and make your life the best it can be even though you have sustained a major loss.

5. Stop believing it was somehow your fault — it wasn't.

6. Learn techniques to deal with triggers — they aren't going away, so learn to handle it.

You are going to find that the basic procedure for recovery is much the same whatever challenges you face. Whether you have to deal with sexual abuse, drug or alcohol addiction, religious abuse, or veteran's issues, the details will differ, but the methods will be similar. Hence, we will be discussing useful tools for just about anybody because everybody faces challenges. These challenges vary mostly by degree. Somebody lied to you, threatened you, ruined your ability to trust, caused you to believe yourself worthless, and/or limited your choices. You are embarking on an epic journey. You plan as well as possible. Choose your companions carefully. You can do this! You will take charge and you will become a thriver if you choose to do so. .

Fear: Both Friend and Foe

My brother once remarked that he didn't understand "why she wants to put herself through all this." He was one of the most fearful people I've ever known even though he swaggered around like he had it all under control. Out of respect for his memory, I will not describe the times he couldn't maintain the façade. I will speak only of myself.

Perhaps it is easier, socially, for women to confess fear. Just like you and every survivor of horrible things, I had hit bottom when I looked for help. Usually, people fear the pain of re-visiting trauma. I am not going to lie to you. It is painful, so painful that many people, like my brother, cannot face it. "Better the devil you know…" runs in their thinking. I am glad I ran off the devils I knew and saved my life.

Fear is debilitating. It can take your life, if not physically, then surely in every other way. You may be the person at the table in a restaurant who is afraid to ask for what she wants, for example, "I'd like no cheese on that." Maybe you think it's too much trouble for the wait staff or the chef to fix food the way you want it within the limits of what is possible. (If the place doesn't sell hot dogs, don't ask for hot dogs.)

You might be the person who does not speak up when something's wrong You may think you are shy or just a "little fish," or that you can't make any difference. You put up with everything, feel bad, and think you are not a real and important person. You may believe that your opinion does not count or that just anybody else knows more than you do. You let the doctor tell you where it hurts. You tell the hairdresser to cut your hair the way *she* thinks it looks best. You spend a lot of time being disappointed in the results you get because you don't know how to ask for what you want. You will learn how to fix that.

Fear stops you from getting the health care you need, sometimes, or taking care of yourself in other ways. You may not wear makeup or find a flattering hairstyle or, if you are a male, you may shave (or not) excessively because in each case, you are afraid to call any attention to yourself. You feel you don't deserve attention, and you are afraid of the reactions it might bring. You constantly want outside confirmation of every decision. You are that person who ends every sentence with "okay?" because you do not trust your own judgment. You also did not get reliable information about how to make choices and decisions. You were to please someone else, not develop as an individual. You were accused of being a tramp or worse if you tried to look nice. Your perpetrator thought you were seeking the attention of someone other than him. You were a bad person for objecting in any way to what the perpetrator wanted. You were terrified of what would happen if you complained at all about anything. You learned denial. I was so afraid of my mother's "care" for me, I never complained of illness. This led to my collapsing at home from strep throat (this was in the olden days, kiddies, before antibiotics). I don't remember having a sore throat. Denial can be that strong even in a young child.

That's where I began to learn the power of mind over body. What we want is cooperation between mind and body, each working with the other to bring about optimum health. What was the result of the strep throat? Well, my mother's favorite child, my brother, had to go stay with our aunt for a week or so until I wasn't contagious. And the story that was told about that illness did not center around what happened to me, but focused on how my brother walked two miles from our aunt's to our house because he missed mom. This was despite the fear of rheumatic fever (it was a real and deadly issue in the days before antibiotics) and the fact that I had extensive testing when I recovered from the strep (I had a rash, so it was scarlet fever) to be sure there was no damage to organs. You probably have some story like that.

You fear loss of control. Abuse is all about power and control. The perpetrator will do whatever is necessary to get complete control over you. Your case may not be as public as Jaycee's or Elizabeth Smart's or Michelle Knight's, but you have been subject to the control of someone who wanted the best for him(her)self, not you. That perpetrator had or has mental health issues that you cannot fix. This person is not going to see you as anything but a possession, an object, a toy. You do not have feelings, wishes, or rights to them. Only extensive mental health treatment can do anything for the perpetrator. He or she will not change without years of work and since he or she does not recognize a problem, this is very difficult. This is why I tell you not to expect the perpetrator to be sorry or ask for forgiveness. The perpetrator blames you. You are right to fear this person. You are wrong to accept that fear as a way of life. People lose their lives by not making this distinction.

My dad took me on "dates" to get treats. He called them dates. I was 4 or 5 and had no idea what a date was. This is often part of the "grooming" process that perpetrators apply to their victims. You may be unfamiliar with this, so a short tutorial is in order. Perpetrators will treat you well at first, supplying you with candy, ice cream, toys or whatever will gain your trust. If you are an adult when this happens—he buys you jewelry or clothes (rarely something like a laptop where you could have access to the outside world and other information). If you do not recognize this behavior, that probably means that the groundwork was laid in your childhood by possibly well-meaning sorts who did not warn you, who kept you "little," or didn't pay enough attention.

Stranger abduction is not typical or common. That's why it makes the papers. About 90% plus of child molestation is perpetrated by someone known to and trusted by the child or the child's family. That makes it easier on the offender who can claim you misinterpreted his actions. You now know to watch out for anybody who tries to isolate you from others. It is a big warning sign when someone wants you "all to myself." Don't be flattered!

Somehow, you have now arrived at a point in your life where you assume control of yourself. If you did not learn to be independent as a child, if you were controlled by parents or teachers or whoever when you should have been learning how to take care of yourself, it will take a while. Clearly, you have learned a lot. Most survivors are able to feed themselves, dress themselves, hold jobs, etc. Outwardly, you would not suspect. However, I have met others who had lost control of their bodies in frightening and socially unacceptable ways. I have met some people who rarely venture out in public for fear of triggers or loss of control. If you fall into that category, there is no way you will be able to gain control without professional help. You did not get the tools to work with as a child.

I was about two years old when my abuse began. Because my parents wanted to present a good front to the world, I was taught how to present a good front. I looked okay; I did well in school; I got more health care than needed. I was not a neglected child. Behind the scenes, I lived in fear. I feared getting whipped, getting treated for my mother's idea of illness, being kept in enclosed places, speaking to anybody about what went on in my home, and expressing any opinion or feeling. I had to learn to express feelings as an adult.

I developed alter personalities which occurs when the mind sections off responses. It is a defense mechanism people use to protect their core personality. You act the part that works long enough that you believe that is really you. I had "Nancy" who managed day to day and in public. I had "Ted," a rebellious teenager. I had "Tank Girl," about seven years old, who protected herself by staying in a military tank all the time, and I had "Linnie," a baby about my age when abuse began. She specialized in hiding, crying, and feeling unloved and betrayed. My "real" personality is who I am today, and if you were to meet me, that is whom you would meet. The alter egos have been honorably retired. They still exist, but they have served well and deserve their rest.

Other people live in fear of you. This may strike you as ridiculous, but it is true. Others are afraid that you will talk about your abuse and survival. This will bring up their own fears. A staggering number of people are abuse survivors because we live in a society where children are not valued. They are expendable. As a group, we are a country of people interested only in themselves. Yes, you will find exceptions galore, but a glance at the headlines will verify this.

There is a reason for all our charities, alerts about animal abuse, and political parties that try to ignore people in need, and that reason is self- centeredness—ego. Most people care about and are willing to work only for themselves and their immediate associates. They are in fear that somehow a good life is going to pass them by. They are afraid something bad will happen, so they store up all they can get against the rest of the world and hang on to it for dear life.

These people think the world owes them something. Now, here you come, saying that you have been treated inhumanely, that you have suffered damaging and unthinkable things, and that you are going to change things, at least, for yourself. The public (even including health care workers) is just as likely to tell you it's "your own dumb fault" as it is to lend you a hand. Why are they like this? They don't want to hear about you for the following reasons:

1. You remind them of all the things they have suffered but have chosen not to address.

2. If they attempt to help you, they will expose their own weakness and be ridiculed.

3. They are afraid you will drain them emotion-ally because their own foundation is so shaky.

4. They might have to make some small sacrifice for you, such as a little time. They would sacrifice only for someone very close to them and, then, only under extreme circumstances.

5. You challenge their weaknesses in taking control of themselves.

Where does this leave you? You must seriously reflect on your own associates. Try trusting them with a little to see what happens. Here's an example: the relative of my cousin asked me for some genealogical information. She assured me that she already had loads of experience and research done. (So why contact me? I thought.) Since I figured she had all this material, I sent her some links to my research and some of the things I had concluded. I mentioned, without going into detail, that the child abuse was a factor, and I wasn't sure my cousin wanted to talk about that although she is aware and has been sympathetic to me and believed me for about 15-20 years.

Back flies an email which says she is VERY close to my cousin, and knows that my cousin would have no part of that. (I did not accuse my cousin of anything except possibly being a victim to some extent.) She, in her lofty position of utilizing a free 14-day trial of Ancestry.com, and using computer exclusively, blew off years of research and documentation by not only me, but quite a number of other researchers, mostly distant relatives. After initial disappointment, I realized that this is the relative my cousin has had the most trouble with, and I now see why. I don't plan, at this time, to contact my cousin. My guess is that my cousin has been positive in talking about her family to this woman and vague. My cousin is good at that and she is very intelligent and self-confident.

Due to my very typical and normal (for a survivor) belief that I have to be perfect, know everything, and express it well in addition to thinking that everybody else knows more (and better) than I do, I felt fear. Fear that somebody didn't like me, that somebody questioned my ability, and fear of public discredit (like writing and publishing a book doesn't open you right up to that!). So what did I do? I replied to the inflammatory email with two statements: "You asked for my information. I sent it." It was difficult for me to re-frame this situation and not act on my initial feelings which were to defend myself, argue for the work I have done, tell her exactly what I think of her (not much), and rat her out to my cousin.

I ended up talking to a trusted friend who knows neither my cousin nor her relative. I may not hear from the relative again which is fine. I am satisfied that my research is as accurate as possible and documented thoroughly. Say what you will, these were not especially nice people. They were not convicted felons nor were they wealthy or prominent. They are not household names and you would be unlikely to know any of them. I did the research mainly for myself.

Fear is the number one problem you will have to face and overcome in your journey to recovery, both your own fear and the fears of others. It is not an appealing subject. You will have to decide which is worse: facing your fears or continuing to live as you currently do. No one can make that choice for you. It helps to have an objective professional to help you through it to the point where you can deal with it on your own. This is not weakness, but strength. Just as you would consult a physician and a trainer at the gym to get your exercise program going, your emotional health and recovery need knowledgeable helpers.

This does not have to be terribly expensive. Take advantage of public agencies. Use your insurance benefits. I do not recommend religious organizations unless you are able to evaluate their programs carefully. Many tend to blame you for the problem or offer too simple, ineffective solutions, or are just as bewildered and scared as you are.

Whatever you do, vet the program or counselor with someone objective and trustworthy such as a women's shelter program, your physician, or a national help network. A list of some of these national agencies is at the end of this book. Follow your gut. If the helping person or agency feels "off" or wrong or they have a pat solution for all situations or they minimize you and your problems, get away immediately and try again.

Examples of ineffective or simplistic "solutions" are rampant. If someone tells you to just pray or confess your sins, they don't know what to do. Some cultures exploit the idea that victims are somehow to blame for whatever happens. They will tell you any number of stories about whatever it was they think you did wrong.

You did nothing wrong. They don't understand sexual abuse. If the therapist asks you to do things that are not possible, that therapist is not paying attention or using any creativity. A specific example of that concerns a friend of mine who was in counseling along with her illiterate father. The counselor wanted the father to fill out some questionnaires and write some essay-type answers to statements, etc. The counselor never understood that the client could neither read nor write.

It may seem obvious to you now, but when you are in pain about what has traumatized you, and you are worried about how you are going to recover from this bad situation, an easy answer might appeal to you,

Recovery is work. It is not easy, and you must not think that anybody has a "right" answer to your situation. Your "right answer" will develop over time as you work on it with people who know how to help you learn to know your true self, and how to guide you in healthy directions. They are out there. Check the credentials and reputation of anybody trying to help you and be sure they do not have ulterior motives.

LINDE GRACE WHITE

Developing Self- Esteem

You have little to no self-esteem. That is a fact you are living with. Coming along shortly are a few indicators of low self-esteem (and I am aware that some of these are culturally inflicted upon women simply because we are female). You will realize that every indicator implies a range of satisfaction. That is, you may be totally unhappy with yourself in an area or very happy with where you are now. There is not a fixed point at which you are perfect. For example, you may want to improve your general health and fitness. There is no ideal weight, amount of exercise, or diet that anyone can say achieves the result that is right for each person. Five feet five inches may be the average height of women in the United States, but is it the correct height? Of course not. It is a measurement that helps to give us a range of height so that buildings and spaces can accommodate the most people comfortably.

When you consider self-esteem, it is subjective. Satisfaction is what pleases you. If you lost 10 pounds and feel good about having done so, you have enhanced your self-esteem. Should everybody in the United States lose 10 pounds? No. It varies from person to person. Some are at their desirable weight, some need to lose more than 10 pounds, some need to gain weight. There is no one right weight, size, or physique although advertisers would like us to think so. Your perpetrator and society at large have collaborated to make you feel that there is always something wrong with you. You are not right in any respect. Your perpetrator wants control of you. Society wants you in a pigeon hole (it's easier to deal with you that way: "You're a woman---gay, red-haired, tall, or whatever-- and THEY'RE ALL LIKE THAT, so we treat them this way") and advertisers want to sell you things.

Your first line of defense is to recognize the things you do well and with which you are satisfied. Even if they are small things such as I brushed my teeth this morning, put them on a list. This is good stuff you accomplished. Eventually you will likely stop congratulating yourself for brushing your teeth daily, but at the beginning, you will reward yourself for every approximation toward your goal. When I was the harried mother of very young children, I would even put things like "wipe the baby's face" on the list even though I would do that at least 5 or 6 times a day. It was something I could mark off as having done. I would also put things on the list that I did once, but they usually stayed done such as "hang up clothes." Things on your list might include items such as "write 2 positive things in my journal" or "spend 10 minutes quietly focusing on a thing I am proud of." You are not going to change a lifelong pattern of thinking about yourself in a week. You will have to practice a new kind of self-talk.

Self-talk doesn't get the attention it deserves. We tell ourselves things about ourselves and the world all day every day. For survivors of trauma, this usually is negative. You have a form of Post-Traumatic Stress Disorder similar to war veterans and crime victims. They don't get much help either if that makes you feel any better. Americans like to think we are all very capable, smart, and equal to anything. This is not true, but some do better than others. How you talk to yourself, how you frame events, and what you choose to focus on makes a huge difference in how you get along. Here is an example:

She Sits Up... After They've Gone

You arrive at work one morning to a message that the boss wants to see you. Hardly anything invokes panic more thoroughly than that. You are immobilized at first. You rack your brain wondering what you've done to provoke a summons from the boss. You assume you will be fired. You spiral down into fear, imagining how you will live with no money coming in. You review every workplace relationship for possible trouble. You go over the last month for any time you might have broken a rule, made a mistake, said something questionable, been late, absent, or anything at all that might bother the boss. By the time you get to the meeting, you've all but got your coat on ready to go aimlessly out on the street.

All of your self-talk concerns all the things you did or might have done wrong. You tell yourself that you don't deserve this job any way. You think you've got it coming. You think you are better than this job. Yes, thoughts like this are contradictory because they are irrational. You are in panic mode which is an irrational state. You tell yourself all kinds of crazy things to push at the panic and to restore some equilibrium to your ego.

I'm not going to tell you what to expect at this point from the meeting, but I am going to tell you a better way to handle the situation. Before you let your initial fears engulf you, sit down and take a couple of deep breaths. Tell yourself to be calm and let your adult self be in charge. Your inner child is responding the way it always has responded to scary or hurtful events. That frightened irrational child cannot be expected to make any good decisions, so tell yourself that the child part of you should take a back seat for now while the adult assesses the experience. There is nothing wrong with the child or with the feelings you experience. The feelings themselves are not in your conscious control, but the way you express them is.

The adult, looking past the feelings, can take inventory quickly to determine what, if, anything, has prompted the call to the boss. The adult can recognize that this is not necessarily a bad thing. I once got called to see the principal of the school where I was teaching to receive a thank you letter from a principal to whom we had returned a special needs child after the child had been in treatment with us for a couple of years. It was nothing to be sorry about. Everyone was thrilled.

You can go through your inventory and think of some responses to various scenarios ahead of time. These responses are not necessarily ones you will actually make. In your self-talk, remind yourself that feelings come and go, that you are in charge of your own behavior, and that you are and will be a capable lovable person regardless of the outcome. Stay calm with the adult in charge. Listen to whatever is said. If it is something negative, be sure you understand what is wrong. You have a number of options if the message is negative. Do not let your hurt or guilty little child run amok at this point. Assess what to do. You can accept whatever they say, you can get help from a union or a lawyer if it is serious enough, you may be able to present evidence that the boss is mistaken (that doesn't mean you still want to work there), or you may be relieved to be out of a bad situation.

Positive self-talk helps you stay in the moment, responding to what really *is*, not to feelings based in past events or messages. Remind yourself that your brain is capable, that you have come this far, and that you will be able to find a good solution to whatever problem you are facing. A key factor is NOT to let your feelings take the lead. You never ignore your feelings, but you do not put them in the driver's seat. Just as you don't let a child under16 drive your car, you don't let feelings drive your responses.

That is what causes a lot of life disasters: letting feelings completely rule without any reasoning from the adult. Think about road rage. Are those adults behind the wheel? No. Those are little children not getting their way. Thousands of similar examples exist. Here are a few more: a physical adult sulks for hours because someone told him/her how that TV show ends. An adult assumes he/she is unloved because another person does not do his/her bidding. Any time we let feelings rule a scene, we leave ourselves open to problems.

As a survivor, your feelings have probably been ignored or dismissed. Therefore, now, you may not recognize them or feel able to control them. All feelings are neutral in the sense that in and of themselves they are neither bad nor good. We interpret them according to how we experience them. A food example will help here. Did you ever see a TV show where somebody eats something most people would consider disgusting? Their ability to eat that item depends on their ability to interpret that action as being good for them. Usually, they will interpret the eating as neutral or good because there is some reward in eating it: money, fame, whatever. An event that makes one person feel happy makes another cringe. Do you like roller coasters? If you do, then you'll have fun riding one. If not, you will be miserable. The roller coaster is neutral. It is not a good thing or a bad thing. It is how you interpret the experience of it.

In order to develop positive self-esteem, you have to learn all about your feelings. I had a hard time recognizing my feelings at all. When I was a child, my mother told me how I felt and did not validate any feeling I had unless it matched what she thought I should feel. For instance, she didn't seem to object to my crying if I scraped my knee because she figured she would hurt, too, if it were she. She also believed there was a limit to how much a scraped knee should hurt. She frequently diagnosed me as ill when I was sad or tired. Or just for no reason I could discern. She said my eyes looked like I felt bad. That taught me not to make eye contact with her. By adulthood, I had learned to mask all feelings, expressed practically none, and was generally confused.

My dad was no help in this department either. He told me we were playing a fun game when he was raping me. This was very alarming because I was not having fun, but at the same time, I did not know what fun was. I did not like what was happening. It hurt. It was frightening. I couldn't breathe. I gagged. He ignored all signals and laughed and enjoyed himself. I was so cute he could hardly stand it. I did not know there were alternative ways for a father to act for many years. I thought all the daddies were like mine. Your experience is probably similar.

It took lots of years in therapy and lots of self-talk to arrive at a workable situation emotionally. I still tend to be stoic, and I often do not understand why other people have such strong feelings about things. Your Barbie doll doesn't either, but she's not actually thinking in the first place. That painted smile stays in place regardless. You can get underway toward dealing with your emotions and developing self-esteem immediately. You begin by noticing your feelings and categorizing them. It helps to keep a journal so that when you become aware of a feeling, you can jot down what you think it is and the circumstances under which it occurred. Since feelings come and go at lightning speed, you are not going to catch all of them. Just stick to the major episodes at first.

Don't try to analyze at this point. You are really just taking inventory. A very simple chart may be useful to you: columns to write the name of the feeling, a check space for good and one for bad, and a space for circumstances. This will speed things up and enable you to review situations later. Put the date on each entry if that helps you. Decide whether you liked the experience of the feeling or not. This will direct you in how to repeat the feeling or avoid it. You are never going to get them all, and you are never going to have total control over them. You are a human being, and no human is able to control all feelings. For years, you have been an object to others, therefore, no feeling or thought you had ever mattered. Now you are developing a sense of what matters to you and reclaiming your status as a worthy human being. You are moving toward learning how to deal with your emotions on your own terms. It helps to have loving support.

That support may take the form of professional help or help from friends, and, occasionally, family depending upon how you see them involved in your recovery. In my case, I got some support from family members who were, in effect, fellow sufferers. They could cry with me, but they weren't much help in my moving on. My brother remembered a few helpful things, but had nothing to give in the way of emotional support as he was just as damaged as I. People from a support group are usually sympathetic and understanding, but they are in the same process as you are. You may have other issues to overcome, too. You may have health issues, addiction issues, social fears, etc.

Until you can develop a measure of recognition and response choice with your emotions, you need a level-headed friend. I was lucky to have several. These were folks who were not fighting the particular battle I was fighting, but they had had some battles of their own. They were willing to devote time to me, and they weren't afraid to hear me. You will find those friends through your counselor who will help you vet the folks already in your life, such as educators or social workers you may encounter. You may find them in your religious group (caveats still apply here), and you will find them in groups whose purpose is to address these problems. All professional people will maintain appropriate boundaries in dealing with you.

Darkness to Light is one well-respected group for survivors. All cities have groups that will help. If you are in a rural area, county-wide or state agencies are there for you such as Prevent Child Abuse America (this will be divided according to state, i.e. Prevent Child Abuse Ohio operates here). Women's shelters usually have groups and, certainly, have resources for you. You will have to exert some effort to connect with others in or out of these groups because people, including you, are focused first on themselves and then, on others, particularly if they are not being paid to work with you. You will have to speak to others, listen to them with genuine interest in their stories, and start adjusting your ability to give and take in social situations. This may be easy or hard for you. You will have to be the judge of that for yourself.

You can expect to experience new and somewhat frightening things as you begin to learn who you really are and to value that person. Your support people will help guide you, help you see yourself from a healthy perspective, and encourage you to express yourself in safe ways. In a group, for instance, you will learn anger management techniques—and you will be angry if you're not already. During some of my worst periods of anger, I had access to small amounts of clay. As I listened to my students read, work on their spelling, or whatever mainly involved my supervision only, I would form a half-inch ball of clay into a penis shape which I would then smash, pinch, break or destroy in whatever way suited me. Since my students were all severely emotionally disturbed and most of them were abused, they paid no attention, but they also had access to the clay. I would encourage them to express their anger, and they had plenty, with the clay. Clay is cheap, malleable, and doesn't hurt most surfaces.

I also made arrangements with friends who owned their own homes to allow me to throw water balloons at the outside of their houses. I would fill a laundry basket with balloons and hurl them as hard as I could at a rough brick wall. I was careful to pick up all the pieces when I was finished. As I was able to give up some of my anger, I would write those thoughts on paper and safely burn the paper in a fireplace or outside away from houses. A metal bowl or waste can works well for this. Eventually, I did not need to physically deal with my anger, but I have learned how to recognize anger, define why I feel angry, and think of ways to deal with it. Anger, like all other feelings, will not go away. The difference is in how you approach it. Today, if a feeling is very strong and self-talk and analysis of the situation doesn't settle me down, I journal or talk to a friend. I would not hesitate, however, to throw a few balloons.

You will discover what it takes for you to master your emotions, but first, you have to learn what they are, name them, and decide the best way for you to handle them. That is a major step toward developing self-esteem. You are looking for your abilities and talents. You are learning to know yourself.

It will be helpful to start observing those things you get right. It will be hard to accept that you do a lot of things right. Society has a false modesty that says that women, in particular, should discount and dismiss positive traits that they have, especially if those traits do not conform to some gender roles. You have undoubtedly learned that you must take a back seat to all men. You should let him win. You should do whatever he says. Any ideas you have should be for his benefit. This is how you were groomed by the perpetrator and what many in society think is okay. More women than ever in history are achieving college degrees, but they still earn about 30% or more less than men in the same career fields. You may have been told that you can't be a doctor, but you can be a nurse. That is just not true. (And this is certainly not to denigrate nurses who need more and better education all the time. More male nurses are the norm now, too.) The gender divide and the arguments about it have been fairly acute for about 45 years. My 45-year-old daughter (who has a master's degree in special education intervention, by the way) tells me she feels very lucky to have grown up with two grandmothers who worked outside the home as well as a mother who also did. I was the second college graduate in the family on my mother's side (her brother had graduated using the G.I. Bill) and the third on the other side as I had two older cousins.

My mother told me that I didn't need to go to college because she just wanted me to be happy (read a married mother with a husband who has a good career). She was one of the most surprised people in the world when I graduated with my degree in English and Humanities. She was even more surprised when I didn't have a child until I'd been married for almost 5 years. He had to get his degree, you know, and I had to keep us fed and clothed. You may not face the same obstacles to success, but you are still facing considerable family and societal obstacles. The general public mostly wants you to shut up and stay out of their way. The fact that you are a survivor of abuse just heightens the experience all women have.

Now, you take inventory again. List your accomplishments, for example: won spelling bee in third grade, graduated high school, can jump double Dutch, make delicious apple pie, can change a tire or the oil in the car, beat another adult at Checkers—whatever you can do well regardless of whether it is on a par with "cured cancer last Tuesday," or "decided to get a rescue dog from the Shelter instead of buying a purebred from a puppy mill." (Mentioning pets, consider how animals were treated by your perpetrator and how they were treated in your home. This will give you astounding insight into your situation, and, maybe, provide you with a steadfast friend who will love you unconditionally.) You will probably be surprised at the things you can do well. Own them. There are things that you know that others can benefit from your knowing. Be aware of what those are. Live confidently in those areas where you know you excel. Right now, your goal is to learn to know yourself by concentrating on all the things you do right.

For many years, I have known that I am a good musician. I am, obviously, not world-renowned for this, but I am competent and enjoy music very much. Music has made my life bearable at times. I am confident that when I sing in a choir, I will do well. I have developed this talent by learning to read music, understanding musical notation, instruction from professional musicians, taking lessons, and so on. I am not a soloist for a number of reasons. You will learn your areas of strength, the things that bring you joy, and the talents you have to add to society and to life at large.

To enhance self-esteem, look the part. By this I don't mean to suggest that you need to spend lots of money on a makeover or a stylist. You only need to value yourself and do your best to bring out your good features. Be clean and tidy about yourself. Experiment until you find a hairstyle that suits you and, above all, pleases you. My mother was obsessed with my having Shirley Temple curls. I don't know what Shirley had to do to get those curls, but I had to have shoulder length hair (that's as far as mine will grow), have this hair washed in the kitchen sink every Saturday, and bobby-pinned into sausage curls which I had to be careful to keep neat until it dried. My hair stayed pinned overnight. On Sunday, the pins came out and the brushing began. By Monday, it was all gone. My mother didn't do ponytails or pigtails. She brushed, but the hair just hung there. As soon as possible, I took charge of my own hair, although my mother loved to give me a permanent—she should have had a Toni doll as a kid, but the doll with hair you could style hadn't been invented yet, nor could the family have afforded it. I had dolls galore because I was living my mother's dream. You should not do anything about your looks that you do not choose to do. You should, however, make your own decisions about hair, makeup, and so on. You are a beautiful person. Please yourself only in this area. As you recover, the smiles will come to your face more readily.

Here, again, set your priorities. If you need your teeth straightened (I had braces at age 42 because my parents didn't think it was important), plan for how to achieve that goal or any other goal that is costly. Be sure it is what you want and not a message from Hollywood or your perpetrator. You will have to look at your face and body for the rest of your life. Make that a good experience by being in control of how you look and feel. If you have neglected your health, now is the time to improve it. Consult your physician, do the tests, and find out what you need. Don't try every diet you see in the magazines or on TV. These advertisers are trying to sell you something. Figure out, with your physician, what it will take to keep you fit and healthy. Walking is great exercise and it is free.

Take prescribed medicine, if you need to, as directed by your doctor. It is not in your doctor's interest to have you get sicker or die. If you die, you are no source of income. If you get sicker, it's bad advertising, so work with your doctor. You are worth taking care of. You deserve to be as healthy as possible. You owe it to yourself to take care of your body because you will not be getting another one. Don't be afraid if you have not paid much attention before. Many bad habits or normal breakdowns can be reversed or improved. Do you junk your car because you have a flat tire? Do you solve a flat tire by slashing the other three? No. You fix the flat. If you have been a smoker, you can stop. If you have used drugs, you can stop. Whatever damaging behavior you have done, you can stop. There are examples of this everywhere.

My brother smoked three packs a day. He stopped. My son used heroin. He stopped. You get whatever help you need, whether rehab or will power or whatever, and do it. You are worth saving. I'll repeat that: **You are worth saving.**

In developing positive self-esteem, you must surround yourself with those people who will support your effort. I used to call these people my Board of Directors. These were folks who cared about me and whose judgment I could trust. Did I just do whatever they told me? No. I would "run things by" them. I would ask them if my ideas sounded right to them. Weighing their opinions with the facts and my feelings, I made my choices, and I have regretted virtually none of them.

Making your own choices is empowering. Up to now, you have likely been told that you weren't smart enough or self-aware enough to make your own choices. Whoever told you that lied. You are entirely capable of making your own choices. You may need to learn self-confidence and you may have to dig for facts. You may want to get some-one else's opinion. Armed with that information, go for it. You develop confidence by starting with small decisions and work your way up. When I first divorced my husband, I had no credit in my own name. I went to a department store and bought a winter coat using the store's credit card which I had applied for. I then paid the bill monthly until it was paid off. I now had a credit history, and the rest was easy. Start small, but start.

The Gnarly Issues of Trust

You're making progress. I should point out, before we go further, that recovery is not a straight line process. You will take small steps forward, and you will slip back. You will feel that you've got your problems solved and something else will come up or a trigger will click in unexpectedly, and you'll think you're back at square one. This is normal. It is also a lot like learning to ice skate. Even Olympian skaters take a fall now and then. Like an Olympic athlete, you must be consistent in practicing your skill. You have to learn new moves, keep up with current research in your field, and refuse to give up when it's hard. You have to get up as gracefully as possible and carry on. You absolutely can do this. You may start out hugging the wall and bending your ankles, but keep going. Eventually, you will be competent.

Learning to trust others will be very hard for several reasons. Here are some of them:

1. At an early age, you found out that many people cannot be trusted.

2. You believe that you are not able to tell who is trustworthy now. You are hesitant to try anything because of your past betrayals.

3. You think you cannot possibly make judgments about people.

4. You are afraid you are too gullible and will make some further tragic error.

We'll deal with these issues one at a time, although your life is a flowing experience, and just like ice skating, we will sometimes have to go a bit back and forth among these reasons.

Here's what has happened to you: for whatever reason, your parents did not protect little you from abuse. This is a fact you must accept. It is difficult for all of us to understand that our parents fail us to some extent, and if you are a parent, you are failing your child to some extent. Being human means not being perfect, having limitations, and not knowing everything, but it also means having the power to overcome many of your own weaknesses and forgiving those of others. Suppose your father was in the military and came home disabled mentally and physically. Does that make him a "bad" father? No. It gives him and you challenges that have to be met with love. Sometimes love means letting go of our image of someone and facing the reality of that person. It sometimes means making peace with what happened in the past and moving on. It can mean cutting people out of your life. You have to decide, with the aid of professional helpers and trustworthy friends, how you best can handle a situation.

Here is an example of what I'm talking about: a woman in recovery from sexual abuse (we'll call her "Sue") faces the Christmas dilemma: should she do the "right (expected, usual)" thing and spend Christmas Eve and Christmas Day with her dysfunctional family or do something that she wants to do? Just to complicate matters, let's throw a 4-year-old son into the mix and remove Sue's transportation. Sue's mother and father are apt to be drunk through most of the holiday, but they want to see the grandson and give him some toys which may or may not be appropriate. They also want to reminisce about the bad old days when the sexual and drinking behavior were even more out of hand, get enraged all over again about what happened in 1990, and lament their fate regarding jobs, government, and the general cussedness of humankind. They want Sue to be complicit, sympathetic, and to congratulate them on the wonderful epic that is their life. They won't mind a bit if she brings more liquor. She has always been a convenient target for them, and if they have stopped abusing her physically, they remember her as an object and are delighted in a sick way that she has provided a new target in her little boy.

Sue has a new and trustworthy friend named Robin. Robin is a survivor and the widow of her abuser. She has come quite far on her journey to wholeness. Sue wants to spend some of the holiday, if not all of it, with Robin, and Robin likes that idea. Robin's two children will stop by to see their mother for a while, and they like Sue, so Robin's family is not an issue. What will Sue do?

There are several possibilities. Sue can go to her parents' place and cave in to their agenda just as she has always done. She will get some emotional satisfaction because things are familiar and hurt as usual. She will expose her son to things she doesn't want him to see or feel, but, she reasons, "That's reality." Sue can refuse to see her parents at all. She can stay home, cook chicken for her son, and watch "Christmas Story" on TV. Her son will spend Christmas Eve with his father who is an okay fellow. When the son comes home, they'll hang his stocking and all that kind of thing.

A third possible scenario is that Sue arranges with Robin to take her to Sue's parents' on Christmas Eve for a limited time. Robin stays or goes to a church service, shops, or whatever for an hour or two, then promptly picks up Sue and takes her home. You can probably think of other possibilities, but I leave it there to emphasize that there are usually multiple solutions to any problem. Your job is to find the one that makes you the happiest. When people have lost your trust, you are only obligated to treat them with the same kindness and consideration you would if they were strangers, and that might be difficult for you at first.

People lose your trust by failing to recognize you as a full living human being. Parents are particularly susceptible to this attitude. They speak of "MY" child as if they got this kid off the showroom floor at the dealership. A child is not an object. Experienced parents will tell you that the child's personality and individuality were beginning to be evident around the fourth or fifth month of pregnancy. My grandson's ultrasounds consistently showed him sucking on his fingers. Most babies do that, but not all. Many babies continue to do that once born, but he didn't. There is very little that we can say is universal for all humans. (If we actually were objects, there would be much more uniformity.) Even identical twins have their differences.

The "MY" attitude reflects, mostly, the trouble that ensues when anybody acquires a child. No matter how much you want the child, no matter what fire you're willing to walk through, no matter how much it hurts your belly or your wallet, no matter if they take her away and you never see her again, there is pain. It is an unforgettable experience however it happens, and it exacts a toll. When you go through so much, it seems natural to think of that child as having been earned by you and, therefore, yours to do with as you see fit. The vast majority of people love their children. Even abusers have a skewed and perverted love for their children. You do not own any other person. Each person is a unique individual with his or her own personality, talents, and abilities. You may be privileged to help an individual learn, grow, and develop, and you may have quite an influence on that person. It is a privilege and a responsibility to be allowed the opportunity to nurture another person, but you do not possess any other person:

not that person's body, not his or her mind, and definitely not that person's soul.

You lost trust in the adults who "dropped the ball" in raising you. It may or may not have been willful on their part, but you are stuck with the results. So, how are you going to handle it now? When my children were born, I didn't consciously recall my own abuse, but I knew that without doubt there would be some things they would not experience—at least not from me. I did not hit my children and neither did their father. It takes longer to teach without physical violence, but it yields a finer product. They do not hit their children (We are seeing the beautiful results of this in two now grown grandsons. As they say in AA: it works if you work it.) We have had our problems, of course, but when you start with a basic foundation of love and positive regard, you can surmount just about anything. If you had had a healthy version of that foundation, you probably wouldn't be reading this book. So, let's talk about what to do now.

You are an adult and, therefore, now responsible for your reaction and response to everything that happens in your life. It is so very tempting to continue to be a victim because that means you can carry on blaming somebody else for your unhappiness. You can indulge all your emotions and not think about other people at all. It is very comfortable because it is familiar. How easy it is to fall back into your old habits. You can no longer allow yourself to be the passive victim. You are the star of your life. Recovery is work. It may be positive work yielding a lot of satisfaction and, yes, joy, but it is still work. Just ask any recovering alcoholic or drug addict. Ask someone who successfully quit smoking. Ask me about recovery from sexual abuse! Marks made on your psychological self do not leave you. They are there in some form forever. The trick is to get that form into something manageable, useful, and healthy.

Let's use the example of an alcoholic who decides to conquer that. For most people, Alcoholic Anonymous is the most successful program ever. Don't harass me with tales of other methods. You will, undoubtedly, be able to find folks who swear they are sober through some other means. I'm not here to debate that. As they say in AA: "It works if you work it." A dry drunk is an alcoholic who does not drink. This person has not made any psychological changes and, usually, does no more than simply refuse to drink. Many sexual abuse survivors are dry drunks in that they block out huge areas of their lives, don't go certain places, stay away from people/situations that might trigger memories, and so on. As an abuse survivor, you understand this completely.

Here is one way in which you differ from an alcoholic. An alcoholic, first and foremost, admits that he/she has allowed alcohol to control him/her. The famous Twelve Steps are the keys to gaining control over alcohol, and they work, but the alcoholic who has been sober for 45 years will tell you: "I am an alcoholic." Temptation will always be around for the alcoholic. You, by contrast, will always be a survivor, but you are not likely to be surrounded by temptation to go back to being a victim. You may fall back because it is hard work to recover and very easy to go back to old patterns of behavior. No matter how horrible it is, at least, the familiar is what you know.

You, too, have to start by admitting that you have been a victim. That sounds easy enough. You can get enraged about that in a nanosecond. Here's the tough part: you have to forgive yourself for being a child, or for complying with a stronger person's agenda, or for not recognizing danger. That is harder than you think because you have to fight an entire lifetime of enculturation which tells you that everybody else is smarter, stronger, cuter, and more worthy than yourself. As you gradually learn that this is not completely true, you realize the enormous number of lies you have been told. Can you trust anybody? At the beginning, you will think not. Now, just as an alcoholic has to adjust to a new world and self- view, you will have to adjust yourself in the same way. If you, sadly, have some other situation such as alcoholism to deal with, you will be heartened to know that there are many elements of recovery that parallel and support each other, so it's not all new material. Nearly all the skills you learn in recovery from one issue will transfer seamlessly to another.

To rebuild trust, you must begin by trusting yourself. That may sound ridiculous until you think about it. How many times have you chosen to listen to that old recording in your head that says you are not worthy? Or the one that says you should give it up because you can't do it? How about the one that says you aren't smart enough, pretty enough, or whatever enough? There's a whole series of old files about how you will never get a break, fate is against you, or you are just plain weak and a waste of space. You are, no doubt, aware of your own version of these thoughts. To some extent, every living person on the planet has heard the negatives about him or herself. Only the arrogant are able to completely shut them off—in public, at least.

When you hear an old familiar negative noise starting in your head, imagine yourself pushing the "off" button. That negative noise is never going to leave you, but you are in charge of whether or not you listen to it. There is nothing wrong with silence while you're looking for positive replacements. I sometimes wake up in the morning thinking of terrible things that are really not likely to happen. For example, I might think I'm developing a fatal illness despite the fact that there is no indication of any problem—but, of course, it IS possible, but, at this time, not likely. Some folks think that if they stub their toe they're going to be laid up for weeks and might need amputation. Not likely. When that happens, I mentally turn off the switch. I get up. I do something mundane such as go to the bathroom or get a drink of water. I look out the window to see if it's sunny or not—anything to distract my mind from the negative thought. If I keep thinking about it, I tell myself the facts: this is a totally unhelpful thought process, there is no reason to think there is any problem, and then I change the subject. I think about something I want to do that day, I decide what to wear; I think about breakfast; I take a shower-- anything neutral or positive. I turn off the recording. In less than 5 minutes (assuming it's a really tough case), I can hardly remember what I was upset about. I don't go over it to try to remember, either. Any negative thought you have will recur unless you stop it. Most likely, nothing awful is going to happen to you today, so there's no point in worrying about things you can't control anyway.

The next step in learning to trust is to accept that you are your own best friend. You won't let you down. Many (dare I say most?) survivors of sexual abuse do not even trust themselves because no matter what they thought or did as a victim, they were told it was no good. Whatever they chose to eat wasn't the right thing or they were forced to eat food they didn't want. Every answer was the wrong answer. Somebody thought he or she could think for you. When I was a little girl, my mother insisted that she could look at my eyes and determine whether or not I was sick. She would say this, and, no matter what, I would deny it because she was, let's say, vigorous in her attack on illness whether real or imagined by her.

I learned several things from this: 1) I can't tell when I'm sick; 2) my feelings are wrong and inaccurate; 3) my opinion, even about myself, doesn't count; 4) I am pretty stupid if I can't even tell if I don't feel well. An illustration: I am 4 years old. I am running around playing as usual, and my abuse, by the way, is well underway. Suddenly, I pass out, mid-run, in the hall. I have no idea what has happened when I wake up on my parents' bed. I don't say anything because my mother has already called the doctor. This was back in the "dark ages" when doctors made house calls. I was terrified as well as feverish. The doctor was never good news. (Years later, I was amazed when my own children were perfectly willing and, occasionally, eager to see their pediatrician. They do a lot better with illness than I do.)

So, there I lay. My head was heavy and hot. I really didn't want to move or talk. The doctor showed up. He diagnosed scarlet fever. This was still a fairly dread diagnosis in the days before antibiotics were available. He ordered a sulfa drug of some sort. I was just relieved there were no bowel cleansing efforts required. All these years later, that illness (and others) informs my whole attitude toward health issues. I enjoy relatively good health now and am seldom sick. One reason is that I pay close attention to my health and keep informed about my body.

My physician once remarked that after my experience as an abuse victim he was surprised that I had carried and delivered 3 babies. (This was possible because I shifted to my alter "Nancy" to deal with the icky parts and my need for control and my desire for the baby turned out to be greater than my fears. Also, my parents were in another state.) If you were as scared as I was, you, too, would be the picture of health today. Terror, I guess, has its uses.

My mother hovered, and she insisted on quiet. She sent my brother to her sister's to stay for a couple of weeks. This, I'm sad to report, really upset her. He was definitely her favorite, as she had earlier on sacrificed me to my dad. I was born to save my brother from our dad who really didn't like the boy. Dad made no bones about it. He did not want a second child, but my mother pulled a fast one on him. "You were lucky," she told me years later, "to be a girl and to look like his people." This is not exactly a confidence builder.

From your experiences of these kinds of things, you have learned to have no self-esteem, no self-confidence, and no respect for yourself. You have already thought of similar events in your own life. Now, start to use them to your advantage. Instead of letting these events continue to scare you and render you helpless, look for what you have learned. These lessons do not have to be believed any more, but need to be revised to suit your purposes today. Perhaps you learned that if you were a good child, Santa Claus would bring you toys. Eventually, you learned some facts about Santa which may or may not have disappointed you. In any case, you haven't thrown Santa Claus completely out, but you have revised your view of Santa. You take the good points and incorporate them into your life today. You do not continue to dwell on the less appealing aspects or sticky wickets that stretch your ability to believe.

What you believe determines what you do. The thoughts that persist in your brain are the thoughts you will act on. Have you ever driven a bumper car? When you do, you will find that you will be driving the way you are looking. You will do this in traffic, too, but it's a lot safer in a bumper car. If you believe you can control the car and are looking toward where you want to go, you will get to the goal. It requires concentration for you to learn to trust yourself in all life situations. You must look where you're going and adjust course where necessary.

When I have to see my doctor these days, I have to focus on the following things:

1. I am in charge of my health and how I feel.

2. I do not have to accept any treatment I do not want.

3. I am capable, and I understand the consequences of refusing treatment.

4. I have a Living Will and directives for my care, so nothing should happen that does not fit my plan.

5. An ounce of prevention is worth a pound of cure.

6. If I don't trust a doctor, I go elsewhere.

7. Even if the conversation is difficult, I have to speak my truth about the situation.

I needed some surgery some years ago. It was medium serious and not an emergency. My doctor kindly went through every step of the procedure with me and explained not only what he would do, but why he would do it. We had some discussion on a few of the steps and I ended up having a more or less customized procedure. Everybody wound up happy.

My mother could, apparently, never do anything like this. She had several surgeries (two similar to mine), yet they were horrible ordeals. She made the most of it, though, and discussed it at length and in detail with her sisters and her friends. They played "General Hospital" for hours and hours. General Hospital is an emotional contest where each player tries to top the other in the arenas of horror and the-ghastly-things-that-happened-to-me with the extra "how the doctor/hospital screwed this up" component. I have to concede that she lived in a day when normal childbirth kept a woman hospitalized for 10 days to 2 weeks or more while today some women are fighting for 48 hours in the hospital after giving birth. Things have changed. My brother spent 2 weeks in the hospital getting his appendix out when he was about 12. My daughter had hers out about a year or so ago and was hospitalized for 26 hours. It could have been less, but she had to wait a couple of hours until someone could pick her up.

You must learn to trust yourself before you can trust others. If you are not sure or your old files are so strong you can't turn them off, you need help. Professional help is quicker and more accurate, but you can accomplish much with friends who love you, but have no investment in your situation. Your counselor, whether professional or not, cannot be getting some thrill from your problem. The counselor cannot have participated in any way in your abuse, and cannot have a treatment or a religious agenda to promote. Your relatives may be fine folks, but they are not likely to be objective. They will either agree too much with your perspective or they will continue to tell you how stupid and helpless you are even if this message is delivered in a friendly tone of voice.

Somebody is out there who will not be shocked, who will listen carefully, and who will help you recover those damaged or lost parts of your precious self. You may have to look hard, but do not overlook social agencies, self-help groups, and so on. Check these potential helpers on line (the library computer is free) and with reliable people who are survivors themselves. If someone seems wrong to you, do not continue to work with them. Trust your gut. It is instinct that warns you of trouble. No matter what reputation someone has or how popular that person is, if your gut says, "No!" get out of there.

You will need to learn who is trustworthy and to trust those who are. Trustworthy people are those who respect you and your decisions. They do not jump in with solutions the second you mention a problem. They listen and occasionally reflect an understanding of what you said. They let you think it through. In the rare situation where they give some advice, it will be something you can check out for yourself. It will be objective, so that you can choose whether or not it is workable for you. Trustworthy people do what they say they will do and do it consistently. They do not have a lot of conditions you have to meet for them to like you. They will continue to like you even if you mess up because they realize you are human. You do not have to test their loyalty or buy their caring. They care for you willingly, but they are not your parents or caregivers. You are under no obligation to obey them. If your goal is to rebel and be difficult, to relive your adolescence or something along those lines, expect them to become scarce in your life. They are human, too, and have a right to their own lives and activities.

Here, I would like to explain a little further about that second to last sentence in the paragraph above. Although this is not a psychology or psychiatry textbook and I am no expert, I do have some practical information to share. It is human nature to try to recreate a familiar comfortable state of affairs in our lives. We go for what we know regardless of whether that is good, bad, or indifferent. We will, unless we consciously do something else, try to achieve that "home" feeling. Here's an example from my teaching career.

Mark was 7 years old with multiple emotional issues and problems adjusting to the world. He had been evaluated for mental illness, etc. and we had the documentation. Official papers, theory, and real world behavior are not necessarily in sync.

In Mark's experience, the only way to be emotionally comfortable was to space out and draw. He would go through notebook after notebook drawing things. He did nothing else for all practical purposes. He was seeking un-involvement because involvement in life was too painful or hadn't worked for him in other ways. Members of his family continued to abuse him in various ways because they did not choose to change their own behavior. To their minds, Mark wouldn't fall into line and be their idea of "normal." When he got to school, he had no way of relating to others except violence in the service of protecting himself. He believed that the best defense is a good offense. He was referred to my class because he tried to cut off another kindergartener's ear with the safety scissors.

Wisely, his teachers recognized a problem when they saw one. This kind of behavior cannot be tolerated. Mark expected that someone would hit him, yell at him, and then put him off in a corner where he could draw. That's what he was used to.

When he came to our school and my class, things changed. We made him leave his handful of sticks and pebbles at the door, but we didn't throw them away. We had him sit in a study carrel, a sort of box made by screens on three sides. He didn't even have to look at other students. We did not comment when he called out words to people who weren't there, but tried to help him focus on what was happening in the classroom. No matter what he did, we consistently followed our rules and treated him with as much dignity, respect, and love as we could. We did not get emotional with him, especially at first. Uproar is what he knew. He kept trying to create uproar so he could be in a familiar frame of mind and feeling.

Mark had voices in his head who told him all kinds of things. He was trying to appease these voices. We were trying to help him quiet those voices and focus on reality. It took years, but Mark turned out to be a success story. It took cooperation and hard work on the part of everyone connected to this beautiful child. Everyone had to change to some degree.

Usually, you will react to others in the way that is most comfortable for you emotionally and you will unconsciously try to duplicate the circumstances under which you grew up in order to achieve that comfort (even if it was not, in fact, comfortable). You want to know that people are consistent and will act toward you the way you expect them to. This is a totally false assumption and useless desire. People will not do as you expect them to left to their own devices. You can provoke them, however, into treating you the way you've become accustomed to being treated. Everyone's individual personality and experiences will be unique to him/her, so though you may think you have a good idea of what someone will do in a particular situation, he/she may not fulfill your prophecy for that occasion.

For instance, I love chocolate and I am diabetic. Knowing that I like chocolate, you would expect me to be happy if you offer me some. Your prophecy is "She'll love it!" I may or may not accept the treat. It depends on the rest of my diet for the day, the level of my blood sugar, and several other factors. Usually, I can have a little, but not always. In social situations, people will frequently offer you some reason for their failure to fulfill your prophecy. Emotionally reactive folks will not always be able to tell you what feels bad or why it feels bad and they either cut you out of the circumstance or assume you know things you have no way of knowing.

In a helping situation involving actual behavior change, and not merely social issues, things are a little different because much of the interactions are out of your awareness unless you bring them to your attention. Here is what is happening. Person A whom you are trying to help, recognizes that you are trying to be good, nice, and so on. Person A senses that this is the way she has been told people should act toward one another, but her experience is very different, so she feels she needs to try you out, as it were, to see if you are one of those nice people who is a pushover and will not require her to change anything or just like everybody she knows. She will, unconsciously, behave toward you as she has behaved toward those in her past (parents, teachers, pastors, whoever) who were supposed to have her best interests at heart and who were supposed to be helping her mature into a functional and happy adult.

For example, let's say Person A was given the job of laundry to do. In many instances (and we'll let this be one), a child is given a job, but given little or no instruction on how to do it. It is assumed by the parent that anybody 10 years old can operate a washer and dryer and knows all the details about how laundry needs to be done. That, of course, is nonsense. When the stakes are a lot higher than some not-optimally-clean clothes, you run into real danger. You read in the paper about parents who think a 3-year-old will be just fine staying home alone with his 1-year-old brother while Mommy runs down to the corner for soda pop and cigarettes.

So, in our example, Person A is told to do laundry. She messes it up in some way. Now the drama begins. People begin to yell, to criticize, to say she's stupid and untrustworthy, and may even slap her around, or threaten her. She can only conclude that she is actually what these people say she is. Now you come along. You offer to help with the laundry and teach her the tricks, but you really don't know what she does or doesn't know. You will encounter, likely, this reaction or something similar: she thinks she now has a patsy to do the laundry and get her off the hook. She continues to mess it up, says she's stupid, etc. (all the things she's heard before). She plays helpless and waits until you get frustrated and leave her, probably angry. She is not surprised when you give up in disgust. Prophecy fulfilled! That's how everybody treats her and you are no different.

Professionals in the field call this transference. The client transfers the feelings and reactions he or she had to authority as a child growing up and as a victim of trauma to the therapist. Therapists are taught how to deal with this and how to help the client move past this to a point where the client can evaluate situations in reality and make conscious choices about how to respond in those situations.

As the helper of a friend, you do not have those qualifications or information, but that doesn't mean you can't be helpful or a friend. It means that you need to understand your limits and urge the person to seek professional help as needed. If you have a person who sincerely wants to change and will make every effort to do so, you can really help and impact that person's life. If you've tried to give up some addiction, be it drugs, alcohol, smoking, soda pop, or whatever, you know how very hard it is. A good friend who will support you in your effort can make a huge difference. That friend, however, cannot be getting anything out of the relationship other than the pleasure of being your friend and enjoying your recovery of the person you are meant to be. You are a person who can give your friend that pleasure.

In AA, that friend is called your sponsor. Sponsors may or may not become social friends. At any point, both people need to recognize that they may be out of their depth in helping or receiving help. The second that "old feeling" intrudes, you must re-evaluate what you are trying to accomplish. It may be that the relationship is tending toward the toxic, and the two of you should part ways. Generally, I do not recommend this type of helping relationship between friends.

If you have the slightest discomfort, consult a professional counselor. This is your life and you cannot allow yourself to return to old patterns. You do not want to defeat the efforts of a friend to heal in attempting to help.

In learning to trust again, you have no choice but to trust the water company to provide a safe and healthy product, and that is but one of a host of outfits you have to trust. You have to trust that other drivers will be using the correct lane, will obey traffic signals, and so on. You know that everyone is not reliable, and that you are not always one hundred percent reliable. Things happen. Distractions occur. You become ill. Any number of things can and will occur outside your control. You can only prepare as well as you can, and hope others have done the same.

Many survivors become Obsessive-Compulsive Disordered or control freaks themselves because they need so much to have something to count on. Some become religious fanatics because they think God is going to protect them from every little problem. Most survivors lose that opinion early on. In my experience, God generally teaches and protects us by offering us many opportunities to learn ways of dealing with situations which is a way of giving us control. So do we give up on God? No. We ask for guidance through our trials, and we use those miraculous brains we have been given for this purpose. We review the experiences of others. These are gifts that God gives us so that we can maximize our life on earth.

You meet people who seem to be trustworthy and kind. Great! You still have trouble, though, because lots of people will appear trustworthy, kind, supportive, and reliable at first, but later prove to be not so. This may or may not be on purpose to bother you, but you have to have some way to tell if this person is a true friend or not. Do not hesitate to cut a person out of your life if that person is not behaving acceptably, is using you, is attempting to lure you into unwise behavior, or just makes you feel "creepy." Expect some to reject you as well because as we are healing, we try out various strategies which will turn off some folks. The strategy is at fault there, not you and not the other person.

Pay attention to the other person's demeanor. Is this person always right about everything? Is the focus on him/her and how he/she views things? Does this person indulge in gossip? I have met folks like this many times in my life, and they are no longer part of my life. There are about 6-7 billion people on this planet, so don't worry about the 25 you might have to reject as toxic to you. I am sorry to report that most of the people in this category where the person's outward behavior totally belies their true nature are folks I met at church. I hasten to say that many of my nearest and dearest also share religious faith with me, but you can't take them all at face value.

My friend, Debbie, whom I did not meet at church, worked with me. She was competent and intelligent. She had connections where I had none. She also had a very, very narrow and conservative religious viewpoint. To me, she seemed to be parroting her pastor, a well-known preacher, constantly. She could not tolerate differences between herself and others. When we went out to eat while on an out-of-town business trip together, she said grace aloud at the table. I was a bit uncomfortable.

The relationship for work reasons needed to continue, but we live in different states, and those states are not contiguous. Over time, I found myself shuddering when her name came up on my email or when I saw her postings on Facebook. They were, to me, unloving, and judgmental excoriations of others. I wrote her a note and unfriended her. There are things about her I like, and I may have to deal with her in the future, but for now, she is off the radar.

A close friend has family members who are abusive because they have mental illness. They abuse themselves, my friend (when they can), and others. There are valid reasons for their behavior, but my friend's health cannot tolerate them. They are avoided and not encouraged to contact her. When there was a death in the family, many of these people did not come to the funeral, did not participate in any way, did not hold their own memorial, and, yet, complained. They had, in many ways, caused much of the trouble that led to the death. This was hurtful to my friend who had overworked in caring for the person who died. Those people are out of my friend's life for all practical purposes.

When I was struggling with a husband who was cheating, some of my "friends" felt it their duty to tell me where they saw him and with whom. "I saw him at the health food store with some woman I don't know." "He was on the tennis court day before yesterday with some dark-haired girl." Some of their children even took it upon themselves to inform my child at a church youth retreat that her father would be going straight to Hell for his behavior. They quoted the Bible to my kid. These are no longer my friends. My ex-husband actually did die a few years later, and I have no idea where he is spending eternity. It's none of my business and not my call where anybody spends eternity.

I'll quote a little scripture to you here: "By their fruits you shall know them." (Matthew 7:16) This is how you decide who is a friend to you and who is not. Proceed with caution when you meet new people. Don't commit yourself too much too soon. Watch them, listen to them, and see if their fruits are the kinds that are healthy and good. You may believe that you should love everybody, and you should be kind as far as possible, but you do not have to hang out with or trust everybody you encounter. The guy at the hardware store is likely just the guy at the hardware store, not your best friend, nor your worst enemy. Despite what you may read or hear or see on television, the great majority of your encounters with others are of no particular importance. Every meeting at the produce section of Kroger will not change your life. Most of life is not very dramatic. If you are expecting that, then you are still suffering from your abuse and need to become more realistic.

She Sits Up... After They've Gone

Maybe you have participated in an exercise like this: you are given a fresh clean sheet of paper. You might be instructed to write something on it or not—really doesn't matter. You are then told to wad that paper up in a tight ball. After that, you open it and smooth it out. Is the paper the same? Can you restore it to the way it was before you wadded it up? This represents you as a survivor. You started out trusting and self-confident. Potential was clear. The abuse happened, and now, you are trying to smooth out the paper that is you. You must accept that you are never going to be the same. You may be wadded up more than once, but smoothing out can still happen, and that paper can be used for a number of other things. It remains genuine paper with strength and usefulness. You cannot rely on anybody to tell you how to smooth out the paper, do it for you (and they'll try), or judge the value of the paper. You will not be doing that for another person, either. You are solely in charge of your own paper. Are you throwing yourself in the trash or are you using that wrinkled paper for art work or padding or noting down important things or something totally new that's just been thought of?

In dealing with others, remember that your paper is just as papery as anyone's. You can do and say things to damage others and they can do the same to you. Neither of you will be the same regardless of your efforts to restore the paper. You have to do your best and move on.

Most of us want to take the easy way out of everything. We want a good life to be handed to us because that's just what we deserve. You have already noticed that that is not going to happen. That is a lie. The purpose of your life and mine is to use the brain, the talent, the situations, and the tools to make something beautiful. When I speak publicly about my book or my abuse, I use a beautiful piece of artwork to illustrate this concept. This artwork is a mosaic platter made entirely of broken china in various colors, sizes and shapes. I actually asked an artist friend to put it together for me, but I am satisfied with it because, of course, it isn't about gluing glass. It's about making the most of the gifts you have been given. You may not think that you've been given anything worthwhile.

Here are some things you've definitely been given even if it doesn't seem true to you now. You may not have developed these gifts to the level you want or that is optimal for you. I present a bit of an ideal for you in the following list:

1. **Life**—you are here in whatever condition you're in. Where there is life, there is growth opportunity. I know someone who has a profoundly disabled child. There was question about how long this child would survive. He had seizures, couldn't walk or talk, and did not seem to comprehend anything. He can now answer questions about himself with nods, smiles, etc. He demonstrates affection. He is able to play with some toys. He feeds himself. His family is pleased with his progress. He has shown that he can learn some things. Any parent of a disabled child will be able to recount the things that child has learned and he will have learned something.

2. **Self-control**—you have that perfected. You know what you need to do to stay in control of yourself and you know if you lose it. Since you know those things, you can deal with others. You always control how you think about your situation, and as you progress, you get better and better at framing ideas to your advantage. You go to a social event but feel uncomfortable there. You can feel trapped or detained and miserable; you can decide to get ill; you can choose to stay and see if things improve; you can find one person to talk to; you can get up and dance; you can leave. There are other options. The point is you control how you react to anything.

3. **Self-worth**—you have learned that because you are still here, you have worth and value. There is a reason for your existence and it is NOT to serve as a bad example! You are here because the universe, or God, or the life force needs your contribution. I am able to help others despite and because of my abuse, but I have other value as well. My children and my writing also give me worth and value, but the fact that you are a human being means you are worthy.

4. **Courage**—You are facing and striking down the most horrible situations daily. You bring secrets to the light of goodness and truth. Your knees may be rattling like castanets, your breath barely equal to a birthday candle, but you are speaking up for yourself and others. Your courage inspires others. Thank yourself for your courage.

Your life is a beautiful mosaic of all your experiences and learnings. What seems useless, damaged, or unworthy still takes its place as part of the whole. Have you decided that some aspect of your life will not be repeated? I determined many years ago that there were some things I would not do in raising my own children.

At the time, I didn't know why I felt that way, but I just knew at a gut level that I would not hit my children nor be overzealous about their health. Each of them has actually expressed to me as adults that they do not, of course, remember any serious physical punishment (there was none), but that they wished, sometimes, that their Dad and I would have just "hit us" and gotten over it. They didn't always like the discussions of wrong-doing that were interminable to them, but usually less than 10 minutes in real time. We talked about what happened and about better choices in the future. It sometimes involved apologies and restoration. It was a bit tedious, I admit, but it enabled the children to make better choices all around, to think about the effect of their behavior on others, and to learn for themselves how to deal with a variety of situations.

I am extremely pleased with the outcome. Have they made mistakes and done some stupid things? Of course. They are human beings. They, however, have learned about themselves and know what their limits are. They are strong and face adversity with courage and heart. That is what loving parents always want for their children—for those children to do better than they did.

You have the opportunity, now, to make your life count for something. You may have children or not, but you influence others daily by what you say and do. A homeless person living on the street makes a statement daily to others. Your life makes a statement. You are responsible for that statement, especially since you know that you are in control of it and have options. You will have to come to a point where you are willing and able to make changes in order to get on with a happier life. These changes will not be easy nor will they necessarily be fun. You probably already know that if you want to lose weight (or gain it) you will have to make major lifestyle changes. There is no magic formula for losing weight, but there are some basic guidelines you can adapt to your own situation.

The same is true for recovery from abuse or any traumatic event(s). You must acknowledge that change must happen. The discomfort of your life must outweigh the comfort of staying as you are. You feel, at first, that you know the Devil, and you think you'd better let well enough alone. Along the same lines, you know that weighing X pounds is impacting your health and happiness. The Devil or the weight has to become too painful to tolerate. This will motivate you to change, but not until you've had enough.

She Sits Up... After They've Gone

I knew I was depressed and unhappy. I had a sense that it was not due to some transitory problem and would not respond well to some quick fix. It began to interfere with my life. I wasn't enjoying things I had previously loved. I saw no positive future. It became too painful to tolerate. I saw my doctor. I went through 3 or 4 therapists until I found someone with whom I could work. I read extensively as I learned what the problem was. I joined a self-help group, kept a journal, wrote, and found true friends who would let me throw water balloons at their houses or burn papers I had written ugly things on in their fireplaces. I drew pictures. I used modeling clay to make figures I then destroyed. I took antidepressants. I got better.

None of this recovery occurred until I was ready for it. You will not lose weight until you are ready to do whatever it takes for you. I had to recognize what abuse did for me. It was somewhat positive because it was familiar, and, indeed, all I had known as a child. It shielded me from all my emotions, so I did not even know what they were. It kept me away from others. It protected me from having to deal with unpleasantness because I could retreat into one of four alternate personas or simply block it out. Your abuse is keeping you from the life you should have and will continue to do so until you decide to change things.

You might think that change was so desirable that I eagerly jumped into it. Not so. I approached it slowly and carefully. ALL of my relationships had to be evaluated and reformed-- all of them, because I was becoming a different person—a person with one personality instead of four. Even my relationship with myself had to change. If you think this took a long time, you are correct. It took me about 8-10 years, and that is a little below the average of about 12 years in therapy. I worked hard on every front I could. Do not let yourself be discouraged by this length of time. I became steadily happier day by day until I realized that I could be happy without intense therapy and that I did not have to devote part of every day to dealing with the aftereffects of abuse. I am not some exotic specimen here. You can do this, too. It's not easy, cheap, or fun, but it is well worth the investment. You are unique and you are worth it.

Your Perpetrator Is Perpetual

Now there's a frightening thought. You have tried or are trying with everything you've got and everything you know or can find out to get rid of the ugly memories. The flashbacks stop your life often and without warning. You know your relationships with others are dicey and subject to constant question. In the world of the survivor of trauma, there are no degrees of injury. If you, God forbid, got burned, your injury would be classified from first to third degree. A surprising number of people are simply not impressed with anything less than a life-threatening, permanently disfiguring third degree burn. You need to understand that even a mild first degree burn that is treated at home still damages your skin, still leads to scarring, and still increases your risk for deadly skin cancer. And it makes you wary around hot things.

Your perpetrator permanently damaged you no matter how mild whatever he did seems. (I will use "he" for the perpetrator for convenience, but be totally aware that many, many perpetrators are female. Jails are full of them and, probably, the most heinous are the women who have murdered children.) Here as on other occasions, you might be tempted to dismiss your abuse. After all, you may not have suffered permanent physical damage. You didn't die. Somebody else had it worse. You may have merely been touched or harassed at work or somewhere. People tell you "Get over it! You're making mountains out of molehills." You are likely minimizing your abuse yourself.

When traumatic things happen to us, there is usually not some knowledgeable person around to take care of us and interpret what has happened. I heard a story on the radio about an Afghanistan veteran. This man had lost both legs in an IED (improvised explosive device) blow up during battle. He was lucky to be with a lot of other people dealing with the same trauma, though some died. His friend was able to pull him out of the situation, and the vet was saved. He eventually named his son after the friend who saved him.

When trauma happens in public and under circumstances where danger is expected, the victim is a hero. We give that victim every help; we restore what was lost as best we can. The particular vet I mentioned above was being interviewed because he had been the handler of a specially trained service dog and had been reunited with his canine buddy who had survived the battle relatively unharmed. The man suffered great trauma, no doubt about it, however, he did have the advantage of being surrounded by many people who knew there was danger and were prepared to deal with it. He is still recovering and that is happening with great support.

His story has a very happy ending. His family welcomed him home as a hero. The government is helping him learn new skills to provide for himself and his family. He should be furnished with all medical and emotional support he needs. We could spend hours debating whether this adequately happens or not, but you and I are going on from here. This story is merely to illustrate how one kind of trauma is handled compared to the trauma of sexual abuse.

Victims of sexual abuse are not hailed as heroes. They are shamed, blamed, and disregarded as if they were worthless. The main reason this happens is fear. Other people are afraid. They think that being exposed to you is going to make something like that happen to them. They are also ignorant (and I use that term in its denotative meaning) and unaware. If you see an accident on the highway, you may look to see what goes on, but you will probably tune out the majority of the details. Only trained personnel can really help.

You read in the paper or see on TV the layperson who attempted CPR, or covered the victim with his coat, or you even hear a lot of criticism of the person if he didn't "help right" and possibly caused further injury or death. A lot of very nice, caring people will pass you by because they are afraid of somehow "getting it on them," do not know what to do, are unaware of the situation, or do not care about you. People can be stunningly selfish in some cases. You are of enormous worth and value and somebody does care, but you are going to have to demand the attention you need.

The factors mentioned above allow perpetrators to function, often, unimpeded. People may be aware that something is wrong, but they are: 1) afraid, 2) ignorant of the damage done, 3) unaware of what is happening, and/or 4) solely focused on themselves. The first notion you will have to give up is that somebody is going to rescue you, comfort you, and beat up the perpetrator once and for all. That happens in your dreams only. There are people who love you and care enough to listen to you, to help you recover, to comfort you, and to help you gather the strength to move ahead with your life. They may not be the people you were expecting to do this, but they are out there all the same and waiting for you to indicate you are ready to recover as fully as possible.

On many occasions, my younger cousin was also molested by my father. Molestation was just an everyday affair for me, but for her, it was sporadic. She didn't like it and complained to her mother. Our mothers were close sisters who were in each other's pockets all the time. When I realized some facts about my abuse, I called my Aunt

Margaret (my mother had died) to ask her what she knew about it. She loved me dearly and was happy to explain a good deal. She hadn't been very pleased with her daughter's complaints, but she didn't comment, didn't call police, and didn't stop sending the kid over to our house. She, too, was subject to abuse from my dad as I learned later. She talked about how my mother had walked in on her daughter and my dad.

"What did she do?" I eagerly asked, thinking maybe mom had made some attempt to stop it that I had forgotten or overlooked.

"Oh," said Aunt Margaret, "she just walked back out."

Of course, I immediately inquired as to why my aunt had continued to let her child stay with us. Her reply was chilling: "I always thought she'd be safe there."

In my family, people who purportedly loved me were afraid, ignorant, unaware, and focused on themselves. You can probably tell a very similar story. It's the story of the pink elephant in the living room for us and those who love us. For the perpetrator, it's the story of the 500 pound gorilla out on the town. (What does a 500 pound gorilla do when he's out on the town? Anything he wants.)

There are lots of explanations for anyone's behavior and humans are capable of justifying anything. We are wired to protect ourselves and our egos. You have probably heard a number of explanations for the behavior of your perpetrator. You may think you have to forgive the perpetrator for that behavior. That is nonsense. This is not Sunday school.

The picture of forgiveness painted by most Christian churches (as I'm not an expert on other faiths, I can't comment on them) shows people reconciled to each other as if nothing ever happened. They'll have you welcoming intimate involvement with the perpetrator who will have magically transformed.

Do not try this on your own because it can be further damaging to you and others. Religion may or may not be helpful in these cases. You should rely on your therapist to help you decide how forgiveness should be accomplished. There is the occasional repentant perpetrator, but that is a great exception. Don't count on it.

Even Jesus told people "Go and sin no more." (This is found in John 8:11, New International Version) He didn't say it is okay for you to keep on doing what you've been doing. He didn't say to pretend it never happened. He never said damage was not done, but he did encourage you to go on from where you are with a renewed spirit whether you're the perpetrator or the victim.

I am not going to talk about Sunday school forgiveness and I am not qualified to talk about what anybody deserves to have happen to them. I am going to talk about how you can achieve some measure of peace and comfort after your experience. <u>This is not a</u> <u>theological</u> <u>work.</u>

I understand that you may want to punish the perpetrator and that your dreams and fantasies about that are somewhat satisfying. I also know that this is not going to happen. Perpetrators may wind up in jail, may commit suicide, may be killed, may be tortured, or whatever, but none of that will make you feel better. The damage is done. You are changed forever, and your experience is never going to leave you. You have forgiven the perpetrator the moment you decide that this experience is not going to define you, is not going to interfere with your on-going life, and is not going to stop you from having friends, lovers, and family. You will have better, more informed, and more positive relationships because you are learning exactly who you are and what it takes to have a life of meaning. You are going to have the life that is right for you, not necessarily materially, but emotionally, mentally, and, to some extent, physically. Reconciling with the perpetrator is not the goal of forgiveness. The goal of forgiveness is to free yourself from the burden the perpetrator has caused you to carry.

I know one person who was able to accept the perpetrator back into her life. He was that rare commodity, a repentant sinner. Through therapy (both the perpetrator AND the victim, separately and together), hours of talk, and the fact that the perpetrator was family, these people were able to move on. The person is still scarred by the experience, still recovering, and still dealing, at times, with other family members who are in denial, just mental, or choose not to see a problem. This is not likely to happen to you. I would hazard a guess that less than 1% of the time this will happen. Usually it is best to cut the perpetrator totally out of your life.

Do not make the mistake of thinking that paying attention to yourself is wrong. A life goal is learning to know who you are, what your gifts and talents are, forming good relationships with others, and knowing what you have to give to the world that benefits you as well. This is complex work, but well worth the investment you make in it. It takes time, and nobody can do it for you. Unless it's something like baking a peach pie, you have to do all the work, sift the advice, and determine your own course of action. A good listener comes in handy here, but **you listen to yourself in the end.** One thing you must do is to put the perpetrator into his rightful place in your life. This may mean different things to different people.

You will have to talk, think, write, and review everything you know about your abuse. This will be painful and difficult. You will have to forgive yourself. I had to forgive myself for being a baby at the time of my abuse. It is not that I could change my status as a two-year-old, but, at first, I still thought that I should, somehow, have been able to overcome an adult man. I stayed in shock for about 40 years, astounded that nobody came to my rescue. I had to forgive my brother, too, for not saying something and had to realize that he, also, was an abused child. I spent years and years believing that somehow I was the crazy one, the troublemaker, the one who didn't measure up. You are not responsible for things that happened to you as a child. You are grown up now, and you can take charge of healing your childhood.

You may have the satisfaction of knowing the fate of your perpetrator. Maybe he didn't get off the hook entirely. Nevertheless, until you put the perpetrator into the section of your brain where the unimportant stuff goes, he will still have power over you even if he's dead. Even though my father died many years ago, I can still bring his power over me back at will. It is my will, now, not to think of him at all unless I must. When I think of him, I try to figure out why I have to think of him at all. Then, if possible, I focus on anything positive I can come up with. Otherwise, I leave him dead.

I took up the hobby of genealogy years ago trying to get information about how my family allowed abuse to continue through generations. I think I have been successful in stopping it at least in my own immediate family. I wish I had scientific facts to answer why abuse was, apparently, okay in my family. I looked at the history of child abuse in society in general, child-rearing practices through the years, and family documents. I've found out a lot of stuff, but it doesn't make me feel any better about my own abuse. You will have to accept the fact that you were betrayed, mistreated, harmed, and scarred because of someone else's poor choices, bad behavior, lack of love, and evil. Once you recognize that these facts cannot be changed, that you are you with the experience, you can become a new creation with all that baggage stored away where it will not be cluttering up your life. Put the perpetrator in a box in that storage room.

Far too much attention is given to perpetrators in our society. It makes a juicier story for the media to focus on the bad guy. The victim is, usually, just an exceedingly average person who has done nothing wrong or even especially interesting in his or her life. Do people accuse the victim of theft of looking "ripe" for it? Is the victim criticized for having gone to the bank on that day and carrying money in a purse or wallet? That is not news. News is that some miserable deprived druggie had the nerve to snatch the purse and slug the victim on the street. Investigating that is far more interesting than finding out that the victim was headed to the grocery to buy milk for her kids. The news may show the victim if she's really banged up and visibly bleeding, but you can count on seeing a picture of the perpetrator, especially if he has a mug shot somewhere or looks seedy. Few or none of these factors are apt to apply to sexual abuse.

My dad taught Sunday school. He served on the church board, held a respectable job his entire life, was never arrested, and looked well-groomed. People in general had no idea what he did, even when he did it to their children. They thought he was a kind of Pied Piper to children. He entertained them, gave them treats, and then got away with as much as possible. He kept pornography in his tool bench in the basement. He was obsessed with sex and harassed women wherever we were. If my mother was out of town, he made lewd and suggestive calls to her sister. This behavior seems to have been acceptable to others in the family. On the positive side, he was an excellent cook, a fine gardener, and could fix any item that broke around the house. He built a boat in our backyard which we used for years on the Ohio River and in various lakes around the state. He was good looking. Not every monster appears scary. You know that for a fact.

Good public behavior, obviously, doesn't count for anything to the victim. It is merely confusing. I asked my ex-husband (to whom I was married over 18 years) what he thought of my dad. My ex was honest. He said, "I thought he was a dirty old man." This was correct, but it was the first I'd heard of it. People may not say anything or do anything because they don't want to upset the apple cart. They are like the parade-goers in the story "The Emperor's New Clothes" where only one child observes that the Emperor is naked in the parade. Nobody interfered because they didn't want to have to prove anything, they didn't want to upset me or my mother, and they didn't want to call any attention to themselves.

I repeat: you will have to fight for yourself. No one will go to bat for you, but many will appropriately support you. Put all concerns for the perpetrator out of your head. Turn him in, if at all possible, but do not keep trying to redeem the situation. Do not be ashamed of yourself no matter how much dirty laundry is revealed. You did NOTHING wrong.

My mother and my brother were appalled and offended by my dad's behavior toward me, themselves, and others, but they were, apparently, helpless with fear. Even though that was a long time ago, conditions in society for reporting and dealing with sexual abuse have not improved to a point where abuse becomes rare. You are on your own, largely, but there are helpers and folks who will love you. Keep looking for them.

You are under NO obligation to love and redeem the perpetrator. You can't do it, anyway, no matter what you do because it is not in your power. A perpetrator can change, but he absolutely has to do it on his own, at his own volition, and with an enormous amount of help. Many perpetrators are abused children themselves who had no help in triumphing over their own victimhood. This kind of situation is a worthy helping field, but it is not for you. Your job is redeeming, reviewing your own life, and moving on.

Some people will attempt to get you to accept responsibility for your victimization. They will gladly point out whatever it was they think you did wrong. ("You should never have gone with that man even if he did play catch with you, was the scout leader, your coach, or your uncle. You should be more careful." The obvious message is that it is somehow your fault that you were a victim.) They are trying to justify some crazy notion they have, their own guilt, or dismiss a serious problem because it disturbs them and they are helpless.

Do not accept anything (advice, opinion, treatment, or statement) that does not feel right to you, does not come from a reliable source (You wouldn't try to get your appendix out unless a board-certified surgeon gave you scientific evidence that it was needed, so why would you take the advice of your unaffected girlfriend or the mystic you found online?). Do not accept help that doesn't clearly lead to your personal progress toward your goals. You have good instincts, you are lovable, and you are equal to this task.

Whatever your perpetrator did will never leave you. You can't put toothpaste back in the tube once you've squeezed some out. Do you think you're a bad person every time you brush your teeth? Can you get your virginity back? Everybody has toothpaste they can't put back, only the size of the mess differs, and the flavor. The great majority of persons have lost their virginity. That is not the end of the world; in fact, there would be no people at all if everyone remained a virgin.

The key to each of these dilemmas is not that the dilemma exists, but that you have to take charge of how you handle the problem. All that has happened in your life so far has brought you to this point. There are no do-overs. You will have to put on your grown up pants, square your shoulders, take a deep breath, and run your own show beginning now.

Pulling Your Triggers

You have many triggers: things that bring the memories back to you instantly. A trigger can be just about anything including a smell, a certain type of light, a casual remark or word—just anything at all that "triggers" an emotional response related to your abuse in you.

One simple trigger for me is the aroma of Aramis aftershave. Whenever I smell that aroma, I spend a few seconds reminding myself that I am a grown up, Aramis itself is innocent, and I am not likely to be raped at this time. Why? My dad wore Aramis a lot. I associate it with him, and it is not a pleasant association.

Triggers will turn out to be a number of things, all of them individual to you. Some triggers are nearly universal, such as the aroma of coffee or baking bread. These mainly provoke positive associations in the majority of people and bring about pleasant memories and feelings. Your reaction is still unique to you, even though many other people may have the same or similar reactions. There will be people who do NOT like the smell of coffee brewing or bread baking, even if the number is relatively few. Those smells, however, are triggers for everyone. Whether it triggers positive or negative interpretations is strictly personal.

Once a man I knew quite well, and about my dad's height, came and sat next to me on a pew in church. This situation was exactly what it sounds like. There was a space next to someone this man knew in church. He sat down.

The only problem was my mental one. I had to stop praying and assess: "Oh, yeah, it's only Jim. This space was empty and the church is full. He doesn't smell of Aramis. All my interactions with Jim have been fine. He is not about to touch me or hurt me in any way—at least not here and now."

That sounds like a lot of assessment, but you will find it takes only seconds, even split seconds, for you to assess a potential trigger. You may only be aware of the effect of your trigger. You feel okay or good about a situation or you feel not okay or bad about it. You might have to think about the situation to realize what really happened there. Emotions are quicksilver, happen in nanoseconds, and require some response from you. Let me break down the church incident for you in order to help you assess your situation.

Church has always been a safe place for me. I emphasize that it is safe for ME, and that not all people find it safe. Aside from my parents, the people I've met at church did no physical harm to me. I often sat next to my father at church (I think my mother wanted him away from my brother, a fact which was just excellent to my brother.)

My experiences at the church in this instance with Jim were all positive and I was an adult. The man was a fellow member with whom I was friendly. I knew his family, and he knew mine. Neither of us viewed the other as anything more than a friend with a common interest: the church. There are no assigned seats in this church.

My point here is that all of this thinking and assessing had to do with my internal processing and nothing external. I had a momentary reaction to the man sitting down. I thought about it, off and on, throughout the service and, obviously, remember it today. It was a powerful trigger to me. I controlled my response that time and nothing came of the incident at all. I hope to help you, in this section, to learn how to recognize, assess, and control your response to the triggers you encounter.

Recognizing triggers is not always as simple as it sounds. Triggers create feelings in a flash at random times and places. There is no real way to predict them or evaluate their strength in advance. You may be able to guess places or circumstances which might trigger you and avoid them, but this is only practical so far.

I do not willingly go certain places because I am apt to be triggered, but sometimes I have to go there. Doctors' offices are an excellent example. Even when the doctor is well-known to me and trusted, even when I know there is not likely to be any new or scary diagnosis or treatment. Even though I know most people are nervous about a doctor visit, my experience with doctors and, especially with my mother and her approach to illness, my anxiety can cause my blood pressure to go up 20 points or more. I am reluctant to mention any symptoms or questions I might have and I get clammy with fear. I think one aspect of my generally good health and healthy practices relates directly to my horror of requiring any treatment.

The doctor was used as a threat to me as a child to get me to do something my mother wanted me to do. I would be dragged along on my mother's visits to the doctor— visits she appears to have enjoyed because she got personal attention. I would sit in the waiting room, smelling the antiseptic smells, listening to a 50s version of canned music from a radio beside the receptionist's desk, and praying that my mother wouldn't run out of her own ailments and bring up any she might fancy I had. It was that or stay home with my father on the off-chance that he wasn't working that day. Staying with him was dangerous as he was my perpetrator.

Sometimes, I was taken to the doctor by Aunt Margaret to serve as a model patient for her daughter. My Aunt Bertie and my grandmother were likely to be along, too, and they chattered away about their various troubles in great and disgusting detail. I was sneaked into hospital rooms to visit relatives and cautioned to keep my feet off the floor so I wouldn't be spotted by some nurse, and told to keep my mouth shut so I couldn't be heard. The smell of rubbing alcohol can be a trigger for me.

From merely being petrified of all medical experiences, I gradually learned how to talk myself out of the total panic response when some issue arose. I schooled myself on good health habits through classes at school and reading. I never complained. I found other things to do or places to be when mother went to the doctor as soon as I possibly could. I got old enough to stay home alone.

I still research symptoms in my *Merck Manual* or online and wait to call a doctor until I am pretty sure what the possibilities are. I have informed my doctors that I am a survivor and am terrified of them. I do as much preventive medicine as is practical or recommended by my physician. I have, so far, been fairly lucky, and I really don't want to hear about other people's health issues because it scares me. (If I really care about you, I will ask you to tell me what you want to about such issues, but when I ask how you are, I generally don't want details.) I do not seek attention by being sick. This is an example of a trigger you might have to actually deal with rather than try to ignore.

The Aramis trigger I mentioned earlier is one I can ignore. I smell it, I briefly feel the fear, and then I remind myself that this is a passing odor and meaningless. You will have triggers that you become able to ignore. You will still register the trigger and have, maybe, 10 seconds of feelings which might include fear, a chill, fright, or some other negative. Then you will recognize a blast from the past and dismiss it. It will still affect you, make no mistake, and bring unpleasantness to mind however quickly it passes, but it will no longer immobilize you or require any special measures to resolve.

In determining what triggers you have to deal with, be gentle with yourself. When you can re-define a trigger, do it. If you are able to associate the trigger with some benign or positive experience, that is so much the better. I no longer respond to a belt which my parents used to hit me and my brother with fear. Now, a belt is an article of clothing which holds my pants up. I have full control of any belts that come my way.

You will need to be alert to yourself. This may sound selfish to you, but, at least for a while, you are going to have to be selfish about how things affect you. When you experience an outbreak of disease, you immediately look for the cause and make changes as you can. I am especially sensitive to soy in any foods. I get very ill, throw up, and am feeling bad for hours, up to a day if I eat anything with soy. Once I figured out what was causing this horrible reaction, I stopped eating soy. Problem solved. Soy is one kind of trigger for me, but it is an avoidable one.

You can and will take similar problem-solving steps to deal with emotional triggers. Pay attention to the circumstances which make you uncomfortable. They may be avoidable. If so, know that and avoid them! For other triggers, develop your way to handle them as I learned how I could best handle doctor visits and Aramis.

Never blame somebody else for your bad feelings. Nobody *makes* you feel anything. Your response to anything is based on a variety of factors. You have, undoubtedly, been in a situation something like this: a child is playing, noisy and giggly. Under most circumstances, you might be enchanted by a beautiful happy child. If you have a headache today or something you must concentrate on, nothing can be more infuriating than a happy noisy child. The child's behavior is neutral. There is nothing inherently wrong with a happy child. You, based on your experience and current status, may be angry, upset, and hurt. It isn't fair. The world, however, does not revolve around any one person. It is not illegal to be happy, sad, crazy, or feel any other emotion.

Here's what to do: analyze the situation and decide what actions you need to take. This action might include: leaving the area, going home, making sure the child is safe and going into another room, not going to the park at that time of day, adjusting your attitude about noise, or any number of other options. You are in control. If you have some responsibility in the situation—perhaps it's your child—then you may need to make better arrangements. Work out a plan with someone reliable to have the child somewhere else for a while. Your spouse might be able to take charge for an hour. You might be able to enroll the child in an activity that amuses the child for several hours a week.

The point here is that you do not have to constantly suffer from triggered feelings. Think about all the associations you have with the trigger event, and start cutting those down to size immediately. The course of action will be apparent. The problem most survivors have in this area is that they do nothing but feel the bad feelings without taking any charge of themselves.

You have had terrible experiences. Those experiences taught you to react in ways that are no longer effective. You did what you had to do to survive. Now, you can re-tune your responses to your current life. You are not a child now. Adults failed you when you were a child. They did not give you the tools to grow with. You must accept that fact and move on from here. A personal example of this is: I wish my parents had allowed me to have braces on my teeth when I was a young teenager. It would have helped me a lot. They did not want to spend the money. Years later, when my dad died and I inherited a small amount of money, I had my teeth straightened. I was an adult then.

As I proceeded through life, I chose what would happen and no longer responded to my parents' advice or their actions unless they directly affected me. My parents suggested I spank my daughter or give her some kind of medical treatment her doctor did not recommend. I did not do any of those things because I am an adult. I learned not to act just on emotion alone. I do my research where I need information, consult experts as needed, and observe how a course of action affects others (one thing I did as a parent was to observe parents I thought were doing a good job and apply those skills in my own life).

You have already observed that some of your reactions are "over the top." That is, you are responding far more intensely than the occasion warrants. Get to the bottom of that even if it is no fun to figure out. Look at how others behave in similar circumstances and decide whether that would be a good tactic for you. You will be surprised at how far a little brave facing of your own reality will take you. I have no trouble resisting food that contains soy regardless of how delicious I know it is. Soy is not a food I can eat and that has been demonstrated more than once. That is my reality. Do I think that nobody should eat soy because I can't? No. I do what I need to do and let others make their own choices. The major issue in dealing with triggers is being able to step away a bit from the emotional response and kick in the rational response.

People are not rational when they are afraid for their lives or fear great bodily harm. These irrational fears affect all people and, in fact, serve as an excellent deterrent to most folks by keeping them safe. Most people carefully observe traffic before they go into the street. The signal may be in your favor, but that doesn't mean that you don't look around you. Somebody else may have decided to ignore the traffic signals. When you suffered your abuse, you were horribly frightened and in fear for your life. No matter what anybody has said or done since, you thought you would die. In my case, I am quite claustrophobic. This is because my father kept a very firm grip on me when he did his thing. My brother recalled my mother saying to my dad, "At least let her wiggle!" He told me this when, as an adult, I asked him what his observations were and what he perceived our mother's reaction to be. I thought as a 30 pound little girl being crushed by a 180 pound man that I would not be able to breathe. I was panic-stricken. I was sure I was dying. My dad was having a good time and telling me that it was all just a game. This is how physical triggers develop in survivors.

The mental roots of triggers include the lies you were told (it's a game; I would never hurt you, etc.) and the threats that were made. A 180 pound man can carry out any threat he makes to a 30 pound child. By consistently lying, by bribes, threats, intimidation, and sheer size, the perpetrator has power. Do not be influenced by those who can't imagine what power an adult has over a child or who thinks that all children are treated well. "Normal" people will be horrified by your story. Their worst nightmares are reality to you and are your reality. This is why you need professional help in dealing with your responses. You are not bad or wrong. You have been brainwashed, injured, and disrespected as a human being. You didn't make a bad choice. You were simply there and vulnerable. Your perpetrator told you whatever would work to get you into his clutches. He played on your sympathies, your natural goodness, and your respect for others. It is no wonder that you are afraid to trust anybody, do not believe even what you see and experience, or believe you are a hopeless case.

You are much stronger, more courageous, and mature than most "normal" people. But like all people who want things to be different in their lives, you have to do all the work.

When people come to the United States from other countries and decide they want to become citizens, it is not a simple process like, say, joining a more informally structured Christian church. You can join a lot of these churches by saying you believe. I was told by a Baptist church in Louisville that I would be a member if I came 3 Sundays in a row. Becoming a U.S. citizen, if you were not born here or did not have U.S. citizens for parents if you were born somewhere else, takes years, study classes, tests, and a ceremony at the courthouse. You became a citizen of a terrible mental, physical, and emotional country not of your choosing when you were abused. You ended up singing a national anthem you didn't know, like, or choose. Now you can choose and I urge you to do whatever you need to do to become a citizen of yourself.

Mental triggers are mainly words and phrases that cause a response in you that is negative. These triggers are neutral. You interpret them as negative because they trigger scary or bad feelings in you as an individual. Others may find the same triggers neutral or pleasant. One of the big mental triggers for me (and I admit to many of my generation) is anything having to do with body waste elimination.

A friend once commented to me that her mother, like mine, was a bowel freak, handing out, and forcing upon the children laxatives, and so on for no particular reason, seemingly, totally at whim. My friend said that she hates orange juice because her mother put castor oil in orange juice, and "you knew what was coming."

Younger people than I will, I hope, have a very different experience. I cringe when I hear anything about these matters. It is a mental trigger that causes me to feel panic, fear, dread, and mortification. I distract myself when even a digestive health yogurt commercial comes on TV. A cause of this mental trigger for me is that I was embarrassed by all body functions because my mother spoke about my body to her friends and relatives. Everyone felt free to tease me, and nothing was held back including odors, how my body looked, any reaction I had. The neighbors discussed my bowels and the fact that I'd had measles at a backyard picnic. I was embarrassed. The talk seemed to go on for hours. I ran into the house early on and did not come back out until somebody came in to get me because the food was being served.

A mental trigger is any word or phrase that can put you instantly back into that powerless childhood mode you experienced when you were traumatized. As you can probably tell, I avoid all words that would really clarify what I'm saying because even thinking them triggers me.

I can't control what others say, so I have learned to discipline my reactions. I'm sure my friend who hates orange juice has long forgotten the incident of telling me, but I haven't. It has been difficult for me to discuss these matters with my physician, but fortunately, fear and dread have combined to give me very good elimination habits and I have not had occasion to take any drastic measures for about 40 years now. I plan to carry on.

You know what your mental triggers are. You will never be totally rid of them. You will need to think of ways to nip your negative reactions promptly by reminding yourself that you are not in the original situation that caused the trigger at first. You must consciously remember that you are an adult and in charge of just about everything that happens to you. You can dismiss those negative thoughts and feelings through an act of your own will. You will, as far as possible, disarm those words by substituting others for use in most situations. You will not use them yourself except in a controlled way. Mostly, you will stay in the moment. In your journal and with your counselor, you may be able to express your emotions and reflect on your response both then and now. What was reality then is not reality now. You are in control of yourself and your life. No one will ever hurt you like that again unless you let them.

When you were a child, you were overpowered, you didn't know what you could and couldn't do for quite some time. An adult lied to you, bribed you, or threatened you. That was then. This is now. You are an adult and can choose your reactions. It will take effort. You will do well in one place and slip back at another time. There is a learning curve, but you are capable of mastering the skills you need. **You are now in control of yourself.**

Remaining in the here and now is important for you to move on. If you allow yourself to respond now as you did when you were a child, you will be frustrated, angry, and injured just as you were then. You have already met people who are unable to enjoy life because they are stuck in their worst moments. They could win any kind of prize and they would feel undeserving somehow. They wouldn't even consider luck as a factor. "If it weren't for bad luck, I'd have no luck at all" the performers used to sing on the old "Hee Haw" television show. These people refuse to allow any good thing to happen or to influence them. That is how deep that early message of worthlessness goes.

Some folks think they are teaching modesty and humility to kids when they tell those kids how bad they are. Not happening. Kids believe what the significant adults in their lives tell them. Parents need to give realistic criticisms about things and situations, not the character of the child. Say, for example, the shoes are inappropriate for the occasion. A parent trying to grow a child into a confident, capable good citizen will say something like: "If you play baseball in those sandals, I'm afraid you might hurt your feet because the sandals don't cover enough of your feet to keep out rocks or to protect you from scrapes and cuts. How about putting on these gym shoes?"

A parent flying by the seat of his/her pants, without thought for the outcomes, might say "You stupid kid! Where is your brain? Put on these gym shoes right now! We're late." Everyone has a moment now and then, of course, but this last response discounts the child totally: he/she lacks intelligence, common sense, psychic abilities (he should know…), and has no respect for adults or the parent, in particular.

You were more in the second category than the first, as a child. Somebody either thought you were simply an object to be used as he/she saw fit or discounted your ability and talent. Not everything can be left for a child to figure out. Many times, adults will say "She won't remember this" or "He won't care" or "Children this age don't…" None of that is exactly true. If you can remember abuse, then that is something that really stood out in your mind. I can remember abuse (I don't like to) and I had no other information to compare it with, so I thought for years that it was normal. Look back over your experience. Figure out what you learned from each incident. Decide if that was a useful and good learning. Then determine how you are going to view it now.

Remember that you control everything about yourself. Nothing about you is immutable, that is, unable to be changed. There is no black or white and nothing set in stone. You choose what to believe about yourself and nobody can interfere. You may have been told that you were stupid or ugly or whatever insult suited the person delivering it, and, furthermore, that what they said was a fact. That may be someone's opinion, but it is not fact. No one can judge you except your Higher Power. You are trying to learn what is true and authentic to believe about yourself. Dolly Parton has said that people have called her a "dumb blonde," but she knows for truth that she is neither dumb nor blonde. You know the essential truth about yourself. Your job is to live your truth.

Remind yourself as often as it takes that you are no longer in the abuse situation, and get all the help you need. Following this section, you will find a short list of places to get help. Use the same methods I explained in the beginning of this book to evaluate the places suggested. It is very important for the resources you choose to ring true to you, to be understandable to you, and to make sense to you. What means the world to somebody else may leave you cold. If you put the words "adults recovering from child abuse" in your browser and add your state, you will come up with thousands of possibilities. These range from the wonderful to the horrible. The ones I list here are ones I have some information about and feel I can recommend. I have annotated these to give you an idea of what to expect. I do not list books to read because there are hundreds and if you put "adult recovery from child abuse, books" in your browser, you'll be able to select the most useful ones for you.

If you have the slightest doubt that you are actually recovering from abuse, then be certain to put the words Adverse Childhood Experiences Survey in your browser.. There, you will find a 10 question, yes or no, questionnaire. If your score is 4 or higher, you need to seriously look into recovery options. You can read the results of the study conducted by The Centers for Disease Control and Kaiser Permanente. The site gives complete details on their findings. The survey is closed as far as your answers adding to the data, but you will benefit from the commentary.

I am also including a couple of "work book" pages at the end of the book to show you how I organized some of my healing data. Don't rely solely on your memory for data because your mind wants to keep the status quo and therefore is very selective in what you will remember and how long you will be able to stay conscious of a memory before it is buried away from your awareness. Because it hurts so much we are likely to direct our attention elsewhere—even to the point of completely closing off some areas of the brain. Hence, alter personalities develop.

My experience has been that I thought I was just very moody at times when I was actually operating in a defense mode characterized as an alter personality. I had one or two friends who could recognize those alters and tell me. I usually knew but, often, did nothing about it. I would recognize later that some part of me was "putting on an act," to protect the sensitive core personality. If you have this experience, you will know what is happening even if you do not use psychological terms to describe it.

Everybody has the occasional dissociative experience. You are driving somewhere you've driven dozens of times. You arrive safely, but have no recollection of the trip because you were thinking about some other topic. A person with "alter personalities" will do this any time a trigger occurs. She may be able to remember something about the current event, but will remember it as you do events in a dream or when you are drunk or otherwise impaired. You will need help in overcoming this situation if this happens to you.

It is not something that happens to all survivors. I bring it up because it is a possibility. Just because some other survivor experiences this, you may not at all. "Alter personality" is merely the body's coping mechanism and defense system protecting your real self. It is not an indication that you are in some way "broken" or abnormal or wrong.

She Sits Up... After They've Gone

If you get a physical illness, say an infection, your body immediately sends its "army," white blood cells, to the infection. The body bolsters this with any antibodies it has for that and if it doesn't have any, it starts making them as fast as possible. If your body's measures are not able to cope as quickly as you want, you need to see a doctor.

About 70% of illness is self-limiting. That is, it will go away eventually on its own (that doesn't mean, however, that you won't suffer or that you won't have aftereffects, scars, or limitations. Most people who contract chicken pox will survive without treatment, but they are likely to have those little round scars and they will not have enjoyed it. They may also have residual complications that show up much later—shingles, for instance.)

Dissociation is not self-limiting. It is part of the 30% of illnesses that require treatment as soon as possible.

If you think you are experiencing disassociation, see a competent therapist. How would you know if that were happening? I always thought I was "moody," or that I had different ways of acting "to suit the occasion or people I was with." Folks will occasionally comment that your behavior seems different, especially if you aren't able to make your transitions quickly enough.

My niece said her father had two modes which she called "good Daddy" and "bad Daddy." She had to learn to tell with which Daddy she was dealing to know how to approach him on any subject. He seemed totally unaware that he was presenting alter personalities both at home and elsewhere. His behaviors in situations outside the home were sometimes embarrassing, infantile, or merely ugly, as well as completely charming, amusing, and kind. People had quite different experiences of him.

If you are getting mixed messages from others or feel very different from one situation to another, you could easily be dissociating to one degree or another.

How much you dissociate varies according to the type and degree of abuse and your ability to overcome it. You will avoid problem places and events as much as possible. You may be the type of person who cannot face anything alone. You may have a personality you drag out for certain occasions like a party personality or a serious discussion personality. You may have a child or children inside you who choose how to act and what to think. If you do, you have an alter. You can learn how to juggle the parts of your personality and combine them into one core. You will not lose anything but fear. You will still be the smart, funny, charming, and capable person you are inside. That person will be in charge of what you do and how you feel.

My experience might help a little here. My core personality spent a lot of time underground, you might say, because I was always worried about how I'd be accepted. I was subject to a lot of ridicule, teasing as a child, and generally discounted as not being a worthy or desirable person.

My alter Linnie is about 3 years old. She is scared of everything and, especially of being hurt. She stays the same all the time, but calls all the feelings. (I will use present tense because while my alters are integrated and no longer rule, they still exist. I consider them honorably retired. They saved my life and I am grateful to them and always will be. They deserve their rest.)

Until I had integrated Linnie, I had the feeling capacity of a 3-year-old who has been abused. I was fearful, primarily. I did not look forward to anything. I did not feel loved or loving. I hid out and approached people very cautiously. Eventually, the adult part of me had to take

Linnie on her lap (figuratively) and love her into calm and peace. My adult had to get safe first, and then she could go about loving and cherishing Linnie until Linnie could stop taking all the responsibility for feelings on herself. This took time and, meanwhile, other alters were conducting my day-to-day life with the help of such parts of the adult/core personality as were accessible.

There is a lot of your core personality available. You just need to remember to connect to it and not let your alters run every factor of your life. Your adult personality is the one in charge always. Someone disabled parts of it and convinced you that you were not capable of thinking for yourself or being a worthy person. Regardless of what they may have said, done or caused to happen, this is not true. You are a lovable and capable person. Period.

If you have alters, each one will have to be loved into retirement. These alters are your friends. They have made it possible for you to come this far. There is nothing wrong with you or them. They have been preparing you for this day when you move from survivor to thriver. You will want to learn what purposes these alters served for you, what they protected you from, and how you intend to cope with this in the future. You will want to thank them very much for all they have done to help and protect you. You will want to tell them that you love them and that you are excusing them to retire and rest now after all that work.

This is not really a one- time experience. You will do this many times as you grow into your real adult self. It will be tempting to fall back into old feeling patterns because they are familiar and may feel "right" to you. If you do, just acknowledge that, and move on. There is no point in blaming yourself for not being perfect or for forgetting a new idea or whatever. Recognize that you are a human being who is learning to be your authentic self. Nothing is going to change your history, but you are going to change your future.

In Conclusion

You are a unique, valuable, and lovable person. You are completely worth the trouble to become your authentic self. This will not be a TV makeover type experience where the lucky winner gets a total surface do over from experts. You will look different as your recovery progresses. You will have experts who have helped you. Your life will change and you can take all the credit. You will be doing all the work. It is our task in life to become fully and truly who we are. I do not say who we were meant to be since I don't know if that concept even exists. What I do know is that we are valuable and necessary to the world, and that we have gifts and talents we are mandated to use for the benefit of ourselves and others. We are here for each other and for the good of the earth. If you are a believer in God, then you know that God does not mean for you to be a waste of space. God (or the Universe or your Higher Power) has you here to realize your authentic self. You are here to gain wisdom and to discover meaning for yourself.

In your life, so far, you have encountered dreadful experiences. People have betrayed you, misused you, lied to you, and simply not cared about you. This has taken many negative forms. We have been talking about sexual abuse here, but any kind of personality-destroying, PTSD-inducing, trust-stealing event can devastate the person. The recovery process is pretty much the same regardless of the cause. Some variation of the Alcoholics Anonymous

Twelve Steps will apply. Here's how I would interpret them for a sexual abuse survivor.

As summarized by the American Psychological Association, the process involves the following:

1. Admitting that one cannot control one's addiction or compulsion;

2. Recognizing a higher power that can give strength;

3. Examining past errors with the help of a sponsor (experienced member);

4. Making amends for these errors;

5. Learning to live a new life with a new code of behavior;

6. Helping others who suffer from the same addictions or compulsions.

These will have to be adapted to suit your situation, but the general process applies to you. The first caveat is this: **you are not responsible for choosing abuse though an alcoholic is responsible for choosing to drink.** Something happened to you, however, and you were powerless. You must recognize and admit that this happened and that you were powerless. Yours is not a case of "you should have known better," or "you didn't listen," or "you should have been somewhere else." We are raised to believe that we have everything in our control at all times, and that if something gets out of control it is our fault. People often blame people who are affected by natural disasters like hurricanes, tornados, etc. "You shouldn't have built a house there, stupid" is the attitude some take. "Why didn't you take proper steps to avoid trouble?" These folks blame the victim to relieve themselves of any negative feelings your experience raises in them.

She Sits Up... After They've Gone

We thrivers have overcome our quick tendency to blame ourselves for whatever happened. Apparently, 2-year-old Me was just irresistible to a grown man. Those white cotton diapers are just amazingly arousing, I guess. Am I, as a baby, the person responsible to "just say no"? I won't accept any blame for that.

It is very useful for survivors to recognize some kind of Higher Power because they need to know that there is something beyond other people to give them strength and meaning. This "something" does not need to be the God of any tradition—that is, Jewish, Muslim, Christian, Buddhist, Atheist, or something else. There is a force beyond you. You can tap into that source in the way that suits you best. Some will find comfort in meditation. Some find it in nature or exercise. Whatever calms you and takes you out of yourself and your surroundings for a while is your Higher Power if it allows you to see and consult your innermost self and find your core wisdom.

Examining past errors and making amends where possible is useful for survivors. It is not your errors that led to your abuse, but those you made in trying to recover that need amending. As you recover, you see where you could have handled things differently had you had more information. You have made wrong choices. That is a fact because everyone makes wrong choices of some degree. We tend to focus on the glaring errors, and you, probably, didn't make any or many of those. You must accept the fact that you are a human being, that you make mistakes. You are not merely a victim of someone else's bad choices, but you are the lead actor in your own life. You make a glaring error when you do not recognize your power over yourself.

You are now working on living a new life. You have found that many things have to change in order for you to move from survivor to thriver. These are deep changes and may be somewhat painful. You may have to leave some people behind as you move on. The alcoholic has to lose his or her drinking buddies and develop sober friendships. The alcoholic has to develop new strategies to cope with situations where drinking is the norm. They do that. You will have to make extensive changes so that you are no longer surrounded by people who feed your feelings of worthlessness and negativity. You will have to give up your crutches.

I knew people in recovery who truly needed to hold that stuffed animal and carry it around with them at times. Eventually, the toy ended up on the bed or in a chair in the corner of the room. The changes take time, sometimes years, but you get happier all the time. Nobody takes a pacifier to kindergarten and, unless there are physical issues, nobody goes to kindergarten in diapers. Consider yourself as a young person growing up. Everything can't happen at once, but over time and with steady effort, your new life will emerge. It will be happy, too, because you will be forming appropriate relationships, making your own choices, and applying all that you've learned.

You will find yourself at some point eager to help others. You will be able to spot other survivors at 20 paces. You won't exactly know how you know, but you will know. You will cherish those who have helped you. Usually, a warm relationship occurs between an alcoholic and his or her sponsor. You will come to the place where you feel confident first in steering a survivor to help and, then, you will be able to listen to another's story without "freaking out." You may not become a counselor or other mental health professional, but you will become that dear and trusted friend the other person needs so much. You will learn not to give advice, but to listen, to share what you have learned, and gently lead others to the kind of care that is suitable for them. You are always the expert on you. You will be helping others to realize their expertise in knowing themselves.

There is light at the end of the tunnel, my friend. Do not give up because it's hard or hurts. You have been through a great deal and it is not simple to solve. Keep remembering that you are lovable and capable. Remember Al Franken's character, Stuart Smalley, on Saturday Night Live? Stuart was the extreme version of the self-help guru. He said "I'm good enough. I'm smart enough. And, gosh darn it, people like me." You aren't Stuart Smalley (thank goodness!), but you are good enough, smart enough, and likeable enough. Hang in there. I and many others are in your corner. You can do this.

A FEW Things You Might Find Helpful

This is, by no means, an exhaustive list. It does not include hundreds of books that could prove a great help to you. It does include reputable Internet sources, most of which can be accessed by other means as well, such as by phone. These are sources that I feel comfortable recommending, but you will have to determine the "fit" for you, and whether the approach is good for you. The list is meant merely as a starting point. As I have said many times before: this is your journey and you have to do all the work to recover. I don't think anybody, upon reflection, really wants a magical, wand-waving solution because, once again, somebody is doing something to you with their own agenda. You must choose healing and find those people and places that can help you. **No one can give you a solution or a formula for recovery. You have to do this yourself.**

Here's some help:

ACES—Adverse Childhood Experience (s)

www.cbwhit.com/ACEs.htm (essay); www.cdc.gov (pages of pertinent facts and information). You can take the survey itself by going to www.cdc.gov/violenceprevention/acestudy/questionnaires.html .

American Psychological Association—general guidelines for choosing a therapist and getting professional help plus information about factors that indicate a need for professional help.

Adult Survivors of Child Abuse—ASCA can be found at www.ascasupport.org, and is a non-profit organization devoted to helping people move from survivors to thrivers. I could not find a connection in Ohio when I looked, but things may have changed. Website has much useful information anyway.

Darkness to Light—1-866-367-3444. They have many resources in your area.

Help for Adult Victims of Child Abuse—www.havoca.org

National Association of Adult Survivors of Child Abuse—www.naacc.org, 1-323-552-6150 gives numbers to call in various parts of the country

Survivors of Incest Anonymous—www.siawso.org is a 12-step program modeled after Alcoholic Anonymous

Three books to start you off:

Bass, Ellen and Davis, Laurie, The Courage to Heal, with workbook. Collins Living, 2008 This is the classic work on this subject. Its original publication was quite a while ago, but they have updated it. The information is basic and, mostly, only the statistics have changed. Available on Amazon

Herman, Judith Lewis, Father-Daughter Incest, President and Fellows of Harvard College, 1981 with update, 2000. Grim as it sounds, you may have to face this fact. Available on Amazon.

Napier, Nancy, Getting Through the Day: Strategies for Adults Hurt as Children, Nancy J. Napier, 1993.

Here are some writing suggestions to get you started on a journal or other helpful writing.

1. There are NO rules for writing a journal. It says what you want it to say. Grammar and spelling do not count. You are the only person who needs to know what it says. There is no certain time or place you must write. There are no other materials needed beyond paper and pen or pencil.

2. Any kind of paper will do. I have both fancy made-for-the-purpose books and school notebooks. Whatever you like to write on and whatever pen or pencil you choose are fine I do some journaling on the computer now, but I do not save it on the computer. I print it out and keep it with my book journals.

3. If you do not trust those around you, keep your writings locked up. I recommend a metal safety box. You keep all the keys with you. It is vitally important, especially in the beginning, to feel that your thoughts and feelings are accessible ONLY to you. This may or may not change later. Meanwhile, protect yourself. You are doing something that feels dangerous. You are tender, but you are making a courageous step forward. Members of your family, roommates, friends will, often, on the pretext of "helping" you, try to read your journal. In fact, they want to argue with you, see what you say about them, or continue to have control of you.

Below are two possible ways to start a journal entry. Use these or anything that works for you.

Today I feel_____.

It makes me want to_____.

I think the reason is_____.

I am going to do_____

or _____happened.

I want to_____.

It feels like_____.

My next step is to_____.

If you choose to write poems or fiction, you can start by webbing. Start with a word that is foremost in your mind. Write it in the center of the paper. Draw a line from the first word to the next word you think of. Do this until you are out of associations. Then organize whatever is relevant into your writing.

Lists have been helpful to me in focusing thinking. A list simply organizes your thoughts.

Charts are useful. They help you see the "big" picture and allow you to observe how thoughts, feelings, and actions are connected.

Statements such as "I believe_____" or _____ is like _____, clear up confused thoughts. Just because you write a statement in order to think about it, you are not obligated to keep it around. The statement can be accepted, rejected, or changed. You decide. Note-taking from books, web sites, or group meetings serves the same purpose as statements.

She Sits Up... After They've Gone

You will find much help when you step up and ask. **You need not be ashamed of anything that happened to you. You were victimized. Now you are fixing that.** You need to be brave. Confidence will come and change will be made. Remind yourself as often as you need to that you are in charge of yourself.

I found it good for a time to have affirmations on slips of paper on my bathroom mirror. These affirmations were things like "I am lovable and capable." "I can do this." "Look at how beautiful you are." "I am a brave, courageous person and I will recover my life." The affirmations you use can be memes from Facebook or the like, compliments someone has paid you, things you need to remember to tell yourself over and over, or anything that is positive. You are affirming good points about you, not considering anything negative. You've already had too much of that.

Wherever you keep them, look at those affirmations every day and say them out loud to yourself. When you determine that you've "got" one, put up another new one. Do not underestimate your ability. You've survived some of the worst things life can dish out. Nobody has experienced what you have, but their similar experiences will help you decide what steps to take to recover your authentic self. I wish you every success and blessing as you journey on.

101

About The Author

Linde Grace White has a bachelor's degree in English and Humanities from University of Louisville and a master's degree in guidance and counseling from Xavier University. More importantly, she has a lifetime of firsthand experience as a survivor of childhood sexual abuse including working with young survivors in a public school setting. She hopes this book will open your eyes and help you become not only a survivor, but a thriver.